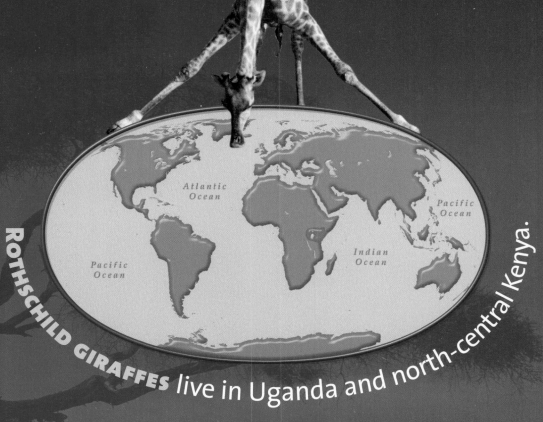

ROTHSCHILD GIRAFFES live in Uganda and north-central Kenya.

Atlantic
Ocean

Pacific
Ocean

Pacific
Ocean

Indian
Ocean

CHARACTERISTIC Giraffes have the same number of bones

in their neck as people do.

CHARACTERISTIC Every giraffe has its own special pattern of spots.

BEHAVIOR Giraffes use their long tongues to get food from tree branches.

HSP Science

SCHOOL PUBLISHERS

Visit *The Learning Site!*
www.harcourtschool.com

HSP Science

Harcourt
SCHOOL PUBLISHERS

ISBN – 13: 978-0-15-360937-4
ISBN – 10: 0-15-360937-0

2 3 4 5 6 7 8 9 10 048 16 15 14 13 12 11 10 09 08

Science On Location Photo Credits
Life: Life Strand Tab (bg) David W Hamilton/Riser/Getty Images; 41 (bg)(tr) Alan Eckert Photography; 43 (bg)(br) Lillian Ledford; 45 (b)(bg) Cody Field Office/Bureau of Land Management Wyoming; (tr) Andrew Kratz/US Forest Service.
Earth: Earth Strand Tab (bg) James Randklev/Taxi/Getty Images; 202 (bg) Millers Custom Photography; (tl) Don Pitcher Photography; 203 (br) Rita Donham/Wyoming Aero Photo; 204 Don Smetzer/Alamy; 205 (t) Don Smetzer/Alamy; 206 (bg) age fotostock/SuperStock; 207 (tr) Frederic Lewis/ Getty Images.
Physical: Physical Strand Tab (bg) Peter Scholey/Robert Harding World Imagery/Getty Images; 380 (bg) William Owens/Alamy; 381 (bl)(tl) Paul Rocheleau/Index Stock Imagery; 382 (bg) Steve Vidler/SuperStock; 383 (cr) Royalty-Free/Corbis; 384 (bg) Robert Perron/AGPix; (cr) Maine State Museum; 385 (bc) Jerry Monkman/IPNStock.com.

Contents

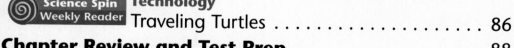

UNIT B Living Together   135

Big Idea
Plants have needs. They have parts that help them live and grow.

Big Idea
Living things have special parts or behaviors that help them survive in their environments. Plants and animals need each other.

Big Idea
Forests, deserts, and oceans are different habitats. Plants and animals have special parts that help them live in these places.

EARTH SCIENCE

UNIT C — About Our Earth — 209

Big Idea
Earth has landforms and bodies of water. Water can change Earth.

Big Idea
People use natural resources, such as rocks and water, in different ways.

Big Idea
We can observe, measure, and describe the weather.

Big Idea
The four seasons all have their own kind of weather.

Big Idea
The sun, moon, and stars are objects in the sky that seem to move because Earth rotates.

PHYSICAL SCIENCE

Big Idea

Matter can be observed, described, and measured. Heating and cooling can change matter.

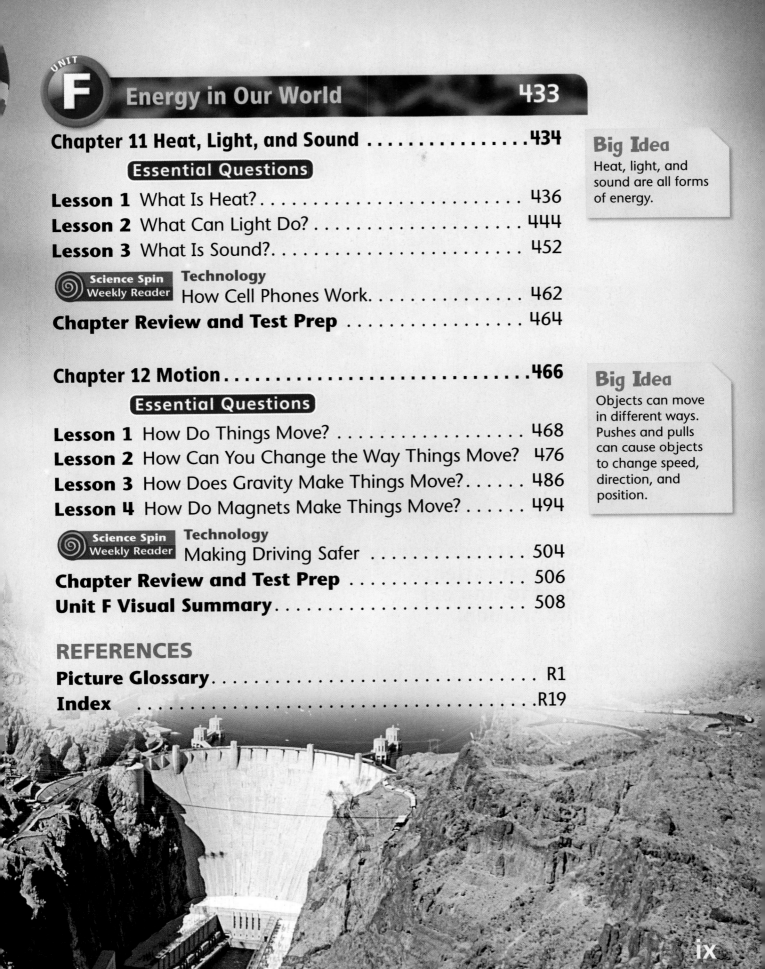

Ready, Set, Science!

What's the Big Idea?

Scientists use inquiry skills and science tools to find out information.

Essential Questions

Lesson 1

How Do We Use Our Senses?

Lesson 2

How Do We Use Inquiry Skills?

Lesson 3

How Do We Use Science Tools?

GO online Student eBook
www.hspscience.com

x

Can children be scientists?
How does this connect to the
Big Idea for this chapter?

Investigate to find out how your senses help you learn about fruits.

Read and Learn about your senses and how to use them safely.

Essential Question

How Do We Use Our Senses?

Fast Fact

Senses
You have about 10,000 taste buds on your tongue! You can use taste and other senses to predict things.

children making
fruit snacks

senses p. 6

3

How Your Senses Work

Guided Inquiry

Ask a Question

How would you use your senses to describe this fruit salad?
Investigate to find out. Then read and learn to find out more.

Get Ready

Inquiry Skill Tip

When you predict, you use what you know to make a guess about what will happen. Use your senses to make predictions about fruits.

You need

oranges

bananas

apples

What to Do

Step 1

Close your eyes. Your partner will give you a piece of fruit.

Step 2

Smell the fruit. Then taste it. **Predict** which kind of fruit you will see when you open your eyes. Was your **prediction** correct?

Step 3

Trade places with your partner. Repeat.

Draw Conclusions

How did using your senses help you make predictions?

Independent Inquiry

Have your partner put an object in a bag. Use all of your senses except sight to **predict** what the object is.

VOCABULARY
senses

 MAIN IDEA AND DETAILS
Look for details about using senses.

Your Senses

People have five senses. The five **senses** are sight, hearing, smell, taste, and touch. You use different body parts for different senses.

 MAIN IDEA AND DETAILS
What are the five senses?

touch

hear

see

smell

taste

Senses Help You

Your senses help you observe and learn about many things.

 MAIN IDEA AND DETAILS

How can your senses help you learn?

What Do You Hear?

Close your eyes, and listen closely to the sounds around you. Predict the sounds you hear. Open your eyes. Were your predictions correct?

7

Senses and Your World

Your senses tell you about the world around you. You can see to know how things look. You can touch to know how things feel. You can hear, smell, or taste things, too.

Focus Skill **MAIN IDEA AND DETAILS** How do your senses tell you about the world around you?

What sound does a bee make?

blooming flowers

Telling About Senses

You can tell how things look, feel, hear, smell, and taste. Do you think that the tree bark would feel rough or smooth? Tell about other things in the picture.

Focus Skill **MAIN IDEA AND DETAILS** **What are some words that tell about the flowers?**

tree bark

How could you describe the birds in this picture?

9

Using Senses Safely

Keep your body safe. Use safety equipment when you need to. Follow the safety rules in the list.

Focus Skill **MAIN IDEA AND DETAILS**

How can you use your senses safely?

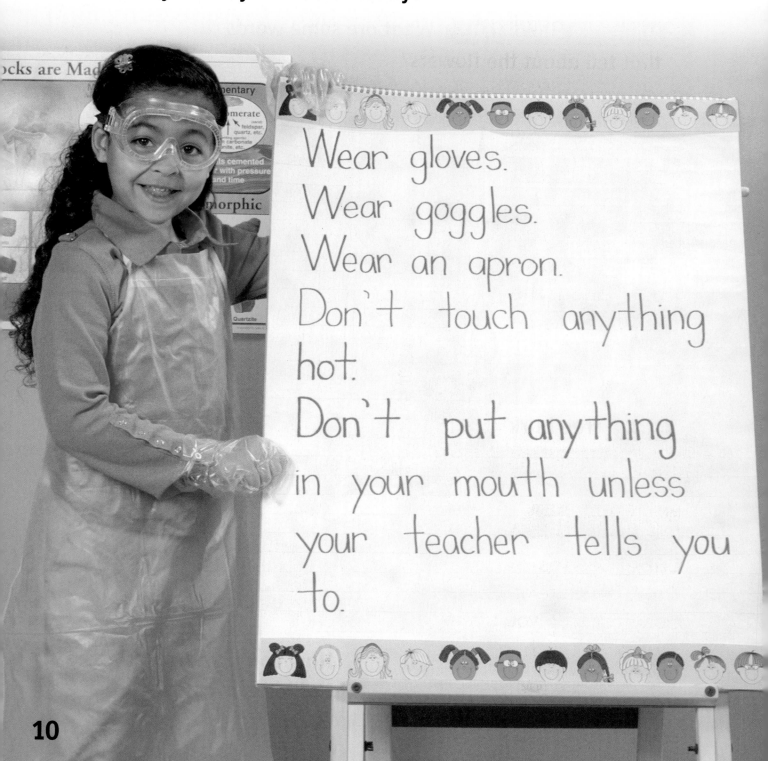

Wear gloves.
Wear goggles.
Wear an apron.
Don't touch anything hot.
Don't put anything in your mouth unless your teacher tells you to.

How do we use our senses?

In this lesson, you learned about your senses and how they help you learn about things.

1. 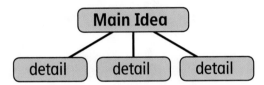 **MAIN IDEA AND DETAILS**
Make a chart like this one. Show details of this main idea. **You have five senses.**

```
        Main Idea
       /    |    \
 detail   detail   detail
```

2. VOCABULARY
Use the word **senses** to tell about the picture.

3. DRAW CONCLUSIONS How can you use your senses to describe things?

4. SUMMARIZE Use the chart to help you write a summary. Tell about senses.

Test Prep

5. Which sense do you use when you feel something?
A hearing
B smell
C taste
D touch

Make Connections

 Writing

Label Senses
Draw a picture of yourself. What body parts do you use to taste, see, smell, touch, and hear? Label the body parts with the correct senses.

11

Investigate to find out why fruits have peels.

Read and Learn how scientists use inquiry skills in their investigations.

Essential Question

How Do We Use Inquiry Skills?

Fast Fact

Peels

Pineapples grow on the ground. They have hard, rough peels. You can draw conclusions about why fruits have peels.

inquiry skills
p. 20

comparing fruits

Fruit Protection

Ask a Question

Observe the watermelons in the picture. Why do you think they need thick peels? Investigate to find out. Then read and learn to find out more.

Get Ready

Inquiry Skill Tip

To draw a conclusion, use what you observe and what you already know to decide what something means.

You need

fruits

hand lens

What to Do

Step ①

Observe some fruits with a hand lens. Look at their peels.

Step ②

Observe the cut fruits with the hand lens.

Step ③

What is inside the fruit?

Draw Conclusions

Draw conclusions about why fruits have peels.

Independent Inquiry

Find pictures of plants. Draw a conclusion about why plants have thorns and bark.

VOCABULARY
inquiry skills

 MAIN IDEA AND DETAILS

Look for the main ideas about the steps scientists use to do their work.

Investigating

Scientists follow steps to test the things they want to learn about.

1 Observe. Then ask a question.

Think of a question you want to answer. What do you want to know?

Is a balloon filled with air heavier than a balloon without air?

2 Form a hypothesis.

What do you think will happen? Write an idea that you can test.

3 Plan a fair test.

Write a plan. List the things you will need to do your test. List the steps you will follow.

Follow the steps of your plan.
Observe. Record what happens.

What did you find out? Was your idea correct? Share your answers. Compare your answers with those of classmates. If you get different answers, do your test again.

MAIN IDEA AND DETAILS What steps do scientists follow to test things?

Using Inquiry Skills

Scientists use inquiry skills when they do tests. **Inquiry skills** help people find out information.

communicate

classify

make a model

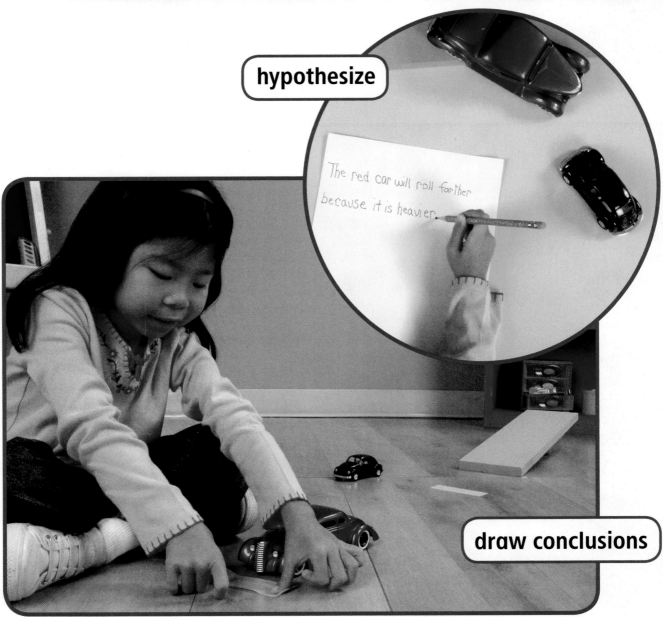

hypothesize

The red car will roll farther because it is heavier

draw conclusions

compare

sequence

measure

GO TEAM!

22

observe

predict

Life Cycle of a Bean Plant

Seed
Sprouting

Seed

Roots

plan an investigation

infer

Insta-Lab

How Far Will It Roll?
Get a ball. Predict how far it will go if you roll it across the floor. Mark that spot with tape. Roll the ball. Was your prediction right?

Focus Skill **MAIN IDEA AND DETAILS**

What skills do scientists use when they do tests?

How do we use inquiry skills?

In this lesson, you learned about the steps and the skills scientists use in order to find out about things.

1. **Focus Skill MAIN IDEA AND DETAILS** Make a chart like this one. Show details of this main idea. **Inquiry skills help people find out information**.

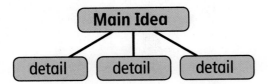

Main Idea

detail   detail   detail

2. VOCABULARY Use the words **inquiry skills** to tell about this picture.

3. DRAW CONCLUSIONS How can a model help you find out about something?

4. SUMMARIZE Use the chart to write a summary. Tell about inquiry skills.

Test Prep

5. What do you do when you compare?

   A make a guess
   B observe how things are alike and different
   C make a plan
   D show how something works

Make Connections

 **Math**

Group Blocks

Get some blocks that are different sizes and colors. Think of ways to classify the blocks. Then classify the blocks in two different ways. Draw a picture of the ways you classified the blocks.

Investigate to compare the masses of different fruits.

Read and Learn about tools that help scientists learn about things.

How Do We Use Science Tools?

Fast Fact

Tools

A blender is a tool that can help make many things—even medicines! You can use tools to compare things.

Vocabulary Preview

science tools
p. 30

using a tool to make
a healthful snack

27

Compare Fruits

Ask a Question

What tool are these people using?

Investigate to find out. Then read and learn to find out more.

Get Ready

Inquiry Skill Tip

When you compare objects, you see how they are alike and different. You can draw pictures to show how you compared the objects.

You need

strawberry

pear

balance

What to Do

Step ① ══════════════════

Put one piece of fruit on each side of a balance.

Step ② ══════════════════

Compare the masses of the fruits. Record what you see.

Step ③

Which fruit has less mass? Which has more mass?

Draw Conclusions

How do you know which fruit has more mass? Explain your answer.

Independent Inquiry

Measure the widest part of two different fruits using string. Compare. Which is bigger around?

VOCABULARY
science tools

MAIN IDEA AND DETAILS
Look for details about
science tools.

Using Science Tools

Scientists use tools to find out about things. You can use tools to find out about things, too. **Science tools** help people do investigations. They help you observe, compare, and measure things.

Some things have parts that are too small to see. You can use a hand lens or a magnifying box to help you see them.

hand lens and
magnifying box

dropper

forceps

You can use forceps
to help you hold or
separate things.

You can use a dropper
to place drops of liquid.

You can use a measuring cup to measure liquid.

measuring cup

thermometer

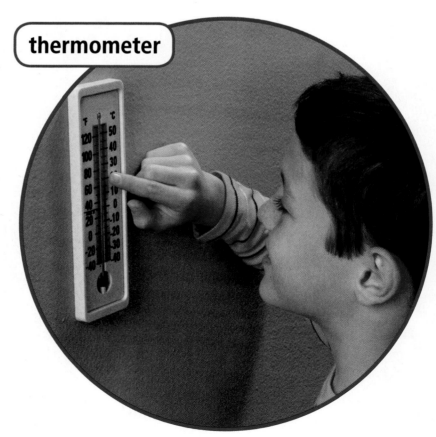

You can use a thermometer to measure how warm or cold something is.

You can use a ruler to measure how long or tall an object is. You can use a tape measure to measure around an object.

ruler

tape measure

You can use a
scale to measure the
weight of an object.

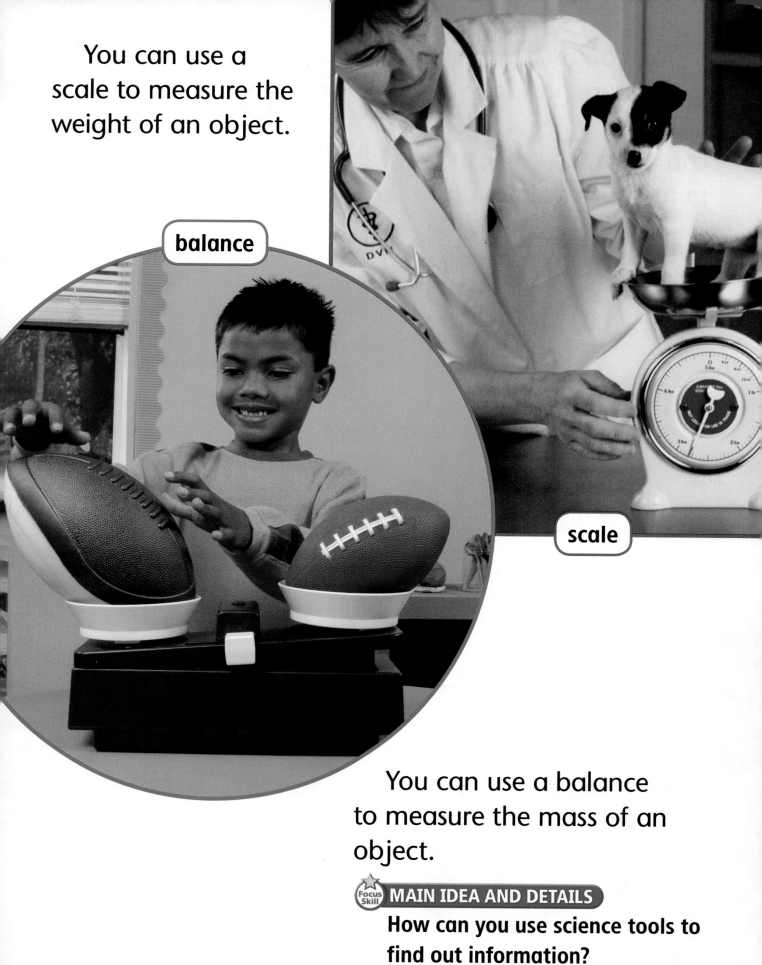

balance

scale

You can use a balance
to measure the mass of an
object.

Focus Skill **MAIN IDEA AND DETAILS**

How can you use science tools to
find out information?

34

How do we use science tools?

In this lesson, you learned how to use science tools to observe, compare, and measure things.

1. 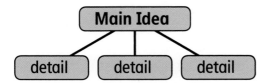 **MAIN IDEA AND DETAILS**
Make a chart like this one. Show details of this main idea. **You can use science tools**.

Main Idea

detail   detail   detail

2. VOCABULARY Use the words **science tools** to tell about the picture.

3. DRAW CONCLUSIONS
Draw conclusions about what you can use science tools to do.

4. SUMMARIZE Tell ways to use science tools to find out about things.

Test Prep
5. Which tool would you use to separate things?
   A hand lens
   B forceps
   C ruler
   D thermometer

Make Connections

123 Math

Estimate and Count
Estimate how many cotton balls it will take to fill a measuring cup. Fill the measuring cup with cotton balls. How many did you need? Was the number of cotton balls more or less than you estimated?

Vocabulary Review

Use the words to complete the sentences.

senses p. 6

inquiry skills p. 20

science tools p. 30

1. **Compare** and **measure** are two _____.

2. Smell is one of your five _____.

3. Scientists use _____ such as droppers and rulers.

Check Understanding

4. Tell **details** about the senses the girl in this picture is using.

5. When you investigate something, what is the next step after you observe and question?

    A do the test

    B form a hypothesis

    C plan the test

    D draw conclusions and communicate what you learned

Critical Thinking

6. Look at these science tools. Which would you use to make something look larger?

Safety in Science

Here are some safety rules to follow when you do activities.

1. **Think ahead.** Study the steps and follow them.

2. **Be neat and clean.** Wipe up spills right away.

3. **Watch your eyes.** Wear safety goggles when told to do so.

4. **Be careful with sharp things.**

5. **Do not eat or drink things.**

LIFE SCIENCE

Nanjemoy Creek Great Blue Heron Sanctuary

Potomac River

Have you ever seen a great blue heron? It is a large wading bird. Each year, many great blue herons go back to the Nanjemoy Creek Sanctuary. It is in Maryland. They return at the same time each year.

Why Herons Go to the Nanjemoy Creek Sanctuary

Great blue herons need the same things other animals need. They need water and food. They need air and shelter. The sanctuary is a shelter for herons. It is away from people. It has all the things the birds need.

The birds go there to have their young. They build their nests in the trees. Females lay from three to seven eggs. The chicks hatch in about 27 days. The young birds are able to leave the nest after 2 months.

mother heron and chick

Think And Write

❶ **Scientific Thinking** What are great blue herons? How are they like other animals?

❷ **Scientific Thinking** Why is this creek an important place for great blue herons?

The Wintergreen Nature Foundation

Do you live in or near Virginia? If you do, check out the Wintergreen Nature Foundation. You get to explore the Blue Ridge Mountains. You can go on hikes. You can search for living things, such as wildflowers, birds, snakes, and insects. You can look at nonliving things, such as rocks and soil.

You can see living and nonliving things in the forest.

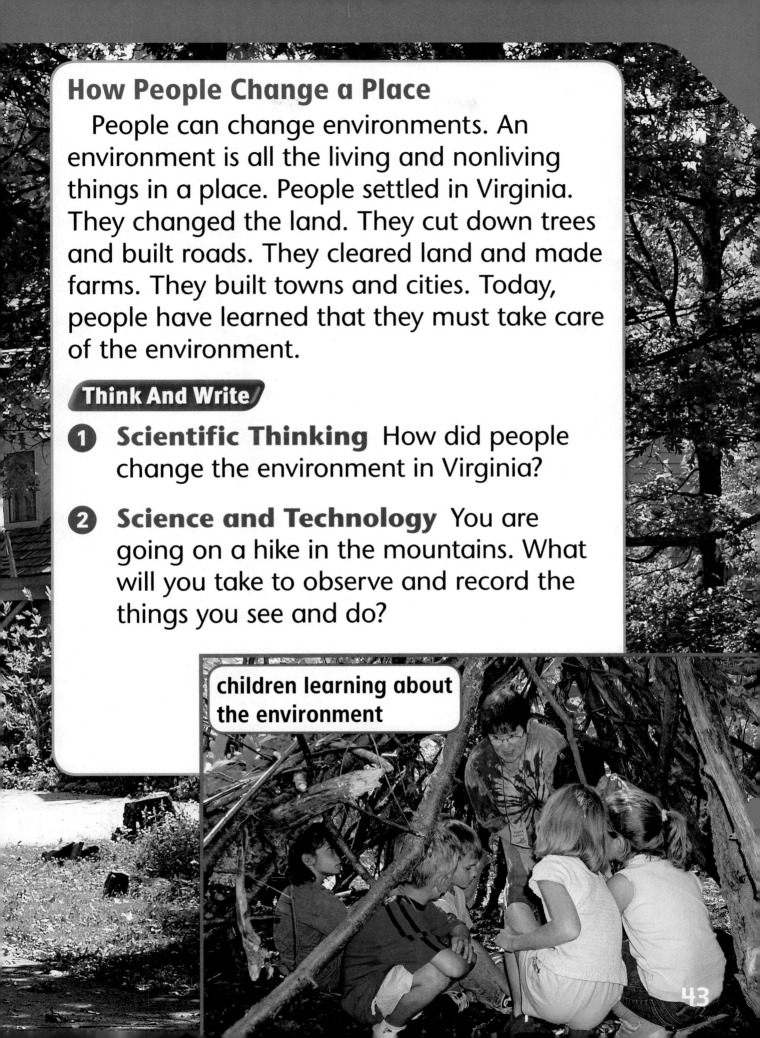

How People Change a Place

People can change environments. An environment is all the living and nonliving things in a place. People settled in Virginia. They changed the land. They cut down trees and built roads. They cleared land and made farms. They built towns and cities. Today, people have learned that they must take care of the environment.

Think And Write

1. **Scientific Thinking** How did people change the environment in Virginia?

2. **Science and Technology** You are going on a hike in the mountains. What will you take to observe and record the things you see and do?

children learning about the environment

43

Five Springs Falls

Have you ever been near a waterfall? It can be very noisy. You can get wet from the spray. Five Springs Falls is a 100-foot waterfall in Wyoming. You can see four kinds of rare plants on the cliff walls around the falls!

Five Springs waterfall

What Plants Need

Plants are living things. They need sunlight, air, water, and nutrients to make food. Some kinds of plants are rare. Others are threatened or endangered. These plants could all die out one day. Four kinds of rare plants live on the cliff walls around Five Springs Falls. There they get what they need to grow. The spray from the falls keeps them moist. They are protected. Hikers are not allowed to climb on the cliffs.

Cary's Beardtongue

Think And Write

1 **Scientific Thinking** What do plants need? Why?

2 **Science and Technology** What could happen to the four kinds of plants if they were not protected? Draw a picture to show how you would protect the plants.

U.S. DEPARTMENT OF THE INTERIOR
BUREAU OF LAND MANAGEMENT

U.S. DEPARTMENT OF THE INTERIOR
BUREAU OF LAND MANAGEMENT

FIVE SPRINGS FALLS
Campground

Project | What's So Special?

You need
- books about animals
- drawing paper
- crayons or markers
- pictures of animals
- scissors
- glue

Koala

The koala sleeps about 22 hours.

What to Do

❶ Each of these animals holds a record. Choose one to research.

ostrich	sloth
giraffe	blue whale
cheetah	capybara

❷ Find out about the animal.

❸ Make a poster. Draw or cut out a picture of the animal. List some facts about it.

❹ Share your poster with your class.

Draw Conclusions

❶ What record does the animal hold?

❷ How is your animal like the other animals?

Design Your Own Investigation

What Plants Need

Do plants need sunlight? Get two plants. Plan an investigation to answer the question. Draw a picture of each plant. Water both plants each day as needed for 5 days. After 5 days, look at both plants. Draw a picture of each one. Compare the pictures.

Plants and Animals All Around

Unit Inquiry

Seeds
As you read this unit, you will find out how seeds grow. Plan and do a test. Find out if seeds need water to grow.

All About Animals

What's the Big Idea?

Animals are living things that have needs.

Essential Questions

Go online

Student eBook
www.hspscience.com

How do penguins meet their needs? How does this connect to the **Big Idea** for this chapter?

penguins on an iceberg

Investigate to find out how living and nonliving things are different.

Read and Learn about living and nonliving things.

Essential Question

What Are Living and Nonliving Things?

Fast Fact

Nonliving Things

Most rubber ducks are made out of plastic, not rubber. Things made out of plastic and rubber are nonliving. You can classify things as living or nonliving.

living and nonliving things

living p. 54

nonliving p. 55

Living and Nonliving Things

Ask a Question

What living thing can you see in this picture? What are some nonliving things in this picture?
Investigate to find out.
Then read and learn to find out more.

Get Ready

Inquiry Skill Tip

When you classify things, you group them by how they are alike. You can draw pictures to show how you classify things.

You need

mealworm

rock

bran meal and box

hand lens

What to Do

Step ①

Put the mealworm, rock, and bran meal in a box. Observe with the hand lens.

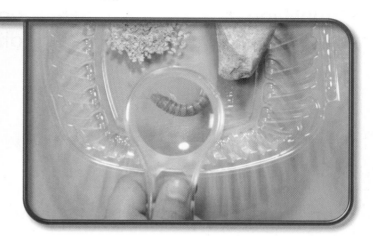

Step ②

Does the mealworm eat or move? Does the rock eat or move? Draw what you see.

Step ③

Classify the mealworm and the rock as living things or nonliving things.

Draw Conclusions

Is the mealworm a living thing? Is the rock a living thing?

Independent Inquiry

Look around the classroom. Pick three things to classify. Record your answers on a chart.

 **COMPARE AND CONTRAST**
Look for ways living things and nonliving things are alike and different.

Living and Nonliving Things

Living things need food, water, and air. They all grow and change. Plants and animals are living things.

Which things in this picture are living? Which are nonliving?

wolf

rocks

54

Nonliving things do not need food, water, or air. They do not grow. Rocks and water are nonliving things.

 **COMPARE AND CONTRAST**
How are all nonliving things alike?

mountain

plants

water

Insta-Lab

Compare Living Things
Look at a living thing. Draw what you see. Then compare your picture with a partner's picture. How are they alike and different? Talk about how you know.

Classify Living and Nonliving Things

You can classify things as living or nonliving. Living things need food, water, and air. They grow and change. If something is not like living things in these two ways, then it is nonliving.

Living	Nonliving

COMPARE AND CONTRAST Look at the chart. How are the living things different from the nonliving things?

Essential Question

What are living and nonliving things?

In this lesson, you learned about how living things are different from nonliving things.

1. **COMPARE AND CONTRAST**
Make a chart like this one. Use it to compare living and nonliving things.

alike — different

2. VOCABULARY Use the words **living** and **nonliving** to talk about the picture.

3. DRAW CONCLUSIONS How do you know a plant is a living thing?

4. SUMMARIZE Use the chart to help you write a summary. Tell about living and nonliving things.

Test Prep

5. Tell how these nonliving things are alike.

ball	cup
rock	water

Make Connections

 Writing

Writing About Animals
Draw a toy animal and a real animal. Label them. Then compare the animals. Write about how they are alike and how they are different.

real bear

toy bear

The toy bear and the real bear are both bears. The toy bear does not need food, water, or air. The real bear does.

Investigate to find out how homes can help animals meet their needs.

Read and Learn about the needs of animals.

What Do Animals Need?

Fast Fact

Caterpillar

A caterpillar eats almost all the time. It sheds its skin when it outgrows it. You can observe how animals meet their needs.

lungs p. 63

gills p. 63

shelter p. 64

caterpillar eating

Observe an Animal Home

Ask a Question

Many birds live in nests. How does this nest help the birds meet their needs?
Investigate to find out. Then read and learn to find out more.

Get Ready

Inquiry Skill Tip
When you observe, you use your senses to find out about things. You can use pictures, numbers, or words to record what you see.

You need

plastic box and gloves

soil, twig, leaf, rocks

water in a bottle cap

small animals

What to Do

Step 1

Put the soil, twig, leaf, rocks, and water in the box. Add the animals.

Step 2

Observe. Draw what you see.

Step 3

Tell how the home you made gives the animals food, water, and a place to live.

Draw Conclusions

How did the animals meet their needs?

Independent Inquiry

Go for a nature walk. **Observe** animals to see how they meet their needs. Record what you observe.

VOCABULARY
lungs
gills
shelter

 MAIN IDEA AND DETAILS
Look for the four things all animals need to live.

Animals Need Food and Water

Animals need food to live and grow. Pandas eat bamboo.

Animals need water, too. Zebras and giraffes drink from ponds. They also get water from foods they eat.

panda

Focus Skill MAIN IDEA AND DETAILS What are two things animals need to live?

giraffe

zebra

Animals Need Air

All animals need air. They have body parts that help them breathe. Giraffes and zebras have lungs. **Lungs** help some animals breathe air. Fish have gills. **Gills** take in oxygen from water.

(Focus Skill) **MAIN IDEA AND DETAILS** What are two body parts animals use to get oxygen?

Pet Food Survey

Take a survey. List some kinds of pet foods. Then ask classmates what their pets eat. Put a tally next to each food. Which foods are eaten by the most children's pets?

Animals Need Shelter

Most animals need shelter. A **shelter** is a place where an animal can be safe. Some birds use a tree as shelter. A hole in the ground is a shelter for foxes.

Focus Skill **MAIN IDEA AND DETAILS**

Why does a bird use a tree as shelter?

owl

foxes

Essential Question

What do animals need?

In this lesson, you learned that animals need water, air, food, and shelter to live and grow.

1. 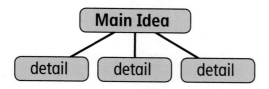 **MAIN IDEA AND DETAILS**
Make a chart like this one. Show details for this main idea. **Animals have needs**.

Main Idea

detail   detail   detail

2. VOCABULARY Use the word **shelter** to talk about this picture.

3. DRAW CONCLUSIONS What are four things that every animal needs?

4. SUMMARIZE Write two sentences about this lesson. Use the words **lungs** and **gills**.

Test Prep

5. What do animals use gills and lungs for?
   A to move
   B to get water
   C to get air
   D to get shelter

Make Connections

 **Math**

Counting Breaths
Count your breaths for one minute after resting. Count your breaths again after running. When did you take more breaths? How many more?

Investigate to find out how animals are alike and different.

Read and Learn about the different groups of animals.

How Can We Group Animals?

Fast Fact

Body Coverings

Feathers help birds fly. They also help keep birds warm. Looking at body coverings can help you classify animals.

Hippopotamuses have hair and birds have feathers.

Vocabulary Preview

mammal p. 70

bird p. 71

reptile p. 72

amphibian p. 72

fish p. 73

insect p. 74

67

Classify Animals

Guided Inquiry

Ask a Question

How are these animals alike?
Investigate to find out. Then read and learn to find out more.

Get Ready

You need

crayons

paper

What to Do

Step ①

Observe different kinds of animals.

Step ②

Draw pictures to record your observations.

Step ③

Classify the animals into groups. Tell how you **classified** the animals in each group.

Draw Conclusions

Why did you classify the animals the way you did?

Independent Inquiry

Look at the animal picture cards. Think of ways to **classify** the animals in each picture.

VOCABULARY

mammal   amphibian
bird   fish
reptile   insect

Focus Skill **MAIN IDEA AND DETAILS**
Look for the main idea and details about each kind of animal.

Mammals

A **mammal** is an animal that has hair or fur. Almost all mammals give birth to live young. The young drink milk from their mother's body.

Focus Skill **MAIN IDEA AND DETAILS**
What is a mammal?

seal and pup

tiger

70

bird feeding chicks

Birds

A **bird** is the only kind of animal that has feathers. Most birds use their wings to fly. Birds have their young by laying eggs. They find food to feed their young.

Focus Skill MAIN IDEA AND DETAILS

How can you tell if an animal is a bird?

peacock

Reptiles and Amphibians

A **reptile** has scaly, dry skin.
Lizards and turtles are reptiles.

turtle

gecko

Most **amphibians** have
smooth, wet skin. Young
amphibians hatch from eggs
that are laid in the water.
As adults, they live on land.
Frogs are amphibians.

Focus Skill **MAIN IDEA AND DETAILS**
What kind of animal has
smooth, wet skin?

frog

red soldier fish

Fish

Most **fish** are covered with scales. Fish live in water. They use gills to take in oxygen from the water.

Focus Skill **MAIN IDEA AND DETAILS**
How do fish take in oxygen?

sailfish

Insects

An **insect** is an animal that has three body parts and six legs. Insects do not have bones. A hard shell keeps their soft insides safe.

Focus Skill MAIN IDEA AND DETAILS How many parts does an insect's body have?

beetle

ants

How Many Legs?

Count the legs of each animal in this lesson. Use the data to make a chart. Then use your chart to compare numbers of legs.

butterfly

How can we group animals?

In this lesson, you learned about mammals, birds, reptiles, amphibians, fish, and insects.

1. 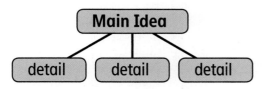 **MAIN IDEA AND DETAILS**
Make a chart like this one. Show details for this main idea. **Animals have different kinds of body coverings.**

```
          Main Idea
        /     |     \
   detail   detail   detail
```

2. VOCABULARY Use the word **bird** to tell about this animal.

3. DRAW CONCLUSIONS
Which two animal groups do you think are the most alike? Explain.

4. SUMMARIZE Write two sentences to tell how animals can be grouped.

Test Prep

5. What kind of animal feeds its young with milk from its body?

  A a bird

  B a fish

  C an insect

  D a mammal

Make Connections

 Art

Patterned Wrapping Paper
Make animal-pattern wrapping paper. Look at patterns on butterfly wings and on other animals. Choose a pattern you like. Copy it onto a large piece of paper. Color it with crayons or paint.

Investigate to find out how adult animals are alike and different from their young.

Read and Learn about the life cycles of different animals.

How Do Animals Grow and Change?

Fast Fact

Mother Polar Bear and Cub
A newborn polar bear weighs less than this book. An adult weighs as much as a car! Compare to see how animals grow and change.

life cycle p. 80

tadpole p. 80

larva p. 82

pupa p. 82

mother polar bear with cub

Animals Grow and Change

Guided Inquiry

Ask a Question

Compare the mother duck with her ducklings. How are they alike? How are they different?
Investigate to find out.
Then read and learn to find out more.

Get Ready

Inquiry Skill Tip
When you compare, you look for ways things are alike and different.

You need

animal
picture cards

What to Do

Step ①

Look at the picture cards. Match each adult animal with its young.

Step ②

Make a chart to **compare** adult animals with their young.

Animals and Their Young		
Animal	Same	Different
sea turtles	Both have flippers.	One is big. One is small.

Step ③

Write about how each adult animal is like its young and how it is different.

Draw Conclusions

Why are adult animals different from their young?

Independent Inquiry

Look in magazines or books for young animals. **Compare** them to see how they are alike and different.

VOCABULARY

life cycle   larva
tadpole   pupa

SEQUENCE

Look for ways each animal changes as it grows.

How a Frog Grows

A **life cycle** is all of the parts of an animal's life.

A frog's life cycle starts as an egg in water. A **tadpole**, or young frog, comes out of the egg. Its tail helps it swim. It takes in oxygen with gills.

eggs

about 7 weeks

about 2 weeks

The tadpole grows legs, and its tail gets smaller. It starts to use lungs to breathe. Soon it is an adult frog. It lives on land most of the time.

Focus Skill SEQUENCE How does a tadpole change as it grows?

about 14 weeks

about 9 weeks

How a Butterfly Grows

A butterfly also starts its life cycle as an egg. A **larva**, or caterpillar, comes out of the egg. The larva eats and grows.

The larva stops eating. It becomes a **pupa** with a hard covering. Inside, the pupa changes into a butterfly. At last, an adult butterfly comes out.

Focus Skill **SEQUENCE** **What happens after the larva stops eating?**

egg

larva

adult butterfly

butterfly comes out

pupa

Insta-Lab

Be a Butterfly

Act out a butterfly's life cycle. What happens first, next, and last? How can you move your body to show what happens?

Animals and Their Young

Dogs are mammals. The puppies look like their parents, but they are not just like them. They are not just like each other. Each puppy is a little different.

How does a puppy change as it grows?

How is it like its parents?

just-born puppies

about 2 months old

adult dog

For more links and animations, go to **www.hspscience.com**

84

How do animals grow and change?

In this lesson, you learned about life cycles. You also learned that animals and their young can look alike or different from one another.

1. (Focus Skill) **SEQUENCE** Make a chart like this one. Tell about the life cycle of a butterfly.

2. VOCABULARY Use the word **tadpole** to talk about this picture.

3. DRAW CONCLUSIONS How is the life cycle of a frog different from the life cycle of a butterfly?

4. SUMMARIZE Write two sentences that tell what this lesson is about.

Test Prep

5. Which animal is a larva and a pupa for parts of its life cycle?

   A butterfly   **B** cat

   C dog   **D** frog

Make Connections

 **Math**

Compare Animal Young

This chart shows the number of young that some animals may have at one time. Use the data to make a bar graph.

Animal Young	
elephant	1
cat	5
owl	6
cockroach	30
crocodile	60

Traveling Turtles
A Trip Across the Atlantic

In late spring, huge sea turtles crawl onto a beach in Florida. Each turtle digs a nest in the sand. The mother turtle then lays about 100 eggs. Two months later, tiny turtles hatch.

The young turtles crawl out of their holes and into the ocean.

A Long Trip

The tiny turtles set out on a long trip. They swim across the Atlantic Ocean and back again. The trip takes between five and ten years. The trip is thousands of miles long.

Scientists wanted to know how the turtles made their way across the ocean. To find out, scientists put "bathing suits" on some young sea turtles. The bathing suits were tied to special machines. The special machines can follow how the turtles swim.

 Think and Write

How long will it take for a young turtle to swim across the Atlantic Ocean?

Find out more. Log on to www.hspscience.com

Vocabulary Review

Tell which picture goes best with each word.

1. mammal p. 70

3. fish p. 73

2. bird p. 71

4. insect p. 74

A  B  C  D

Check Understanding

5. Show the **sequence**. Write **first**, **next**, **then**, and **last**.

(Focus Skill)

A  B  C  D

6. Which is **true** about frogs?

   A They are fish.

   B They have scaly, dry skin.

   C The young are called tadpoles.

   D Adults breathe with gills.

Critical Thinking

7. Compare the pigs. Which one is living? Which is not? Tell how you know.

8. Think about a pet you want. Draw a picture of the pet. List each thing it needs. Tell how you would help it meet its needs.

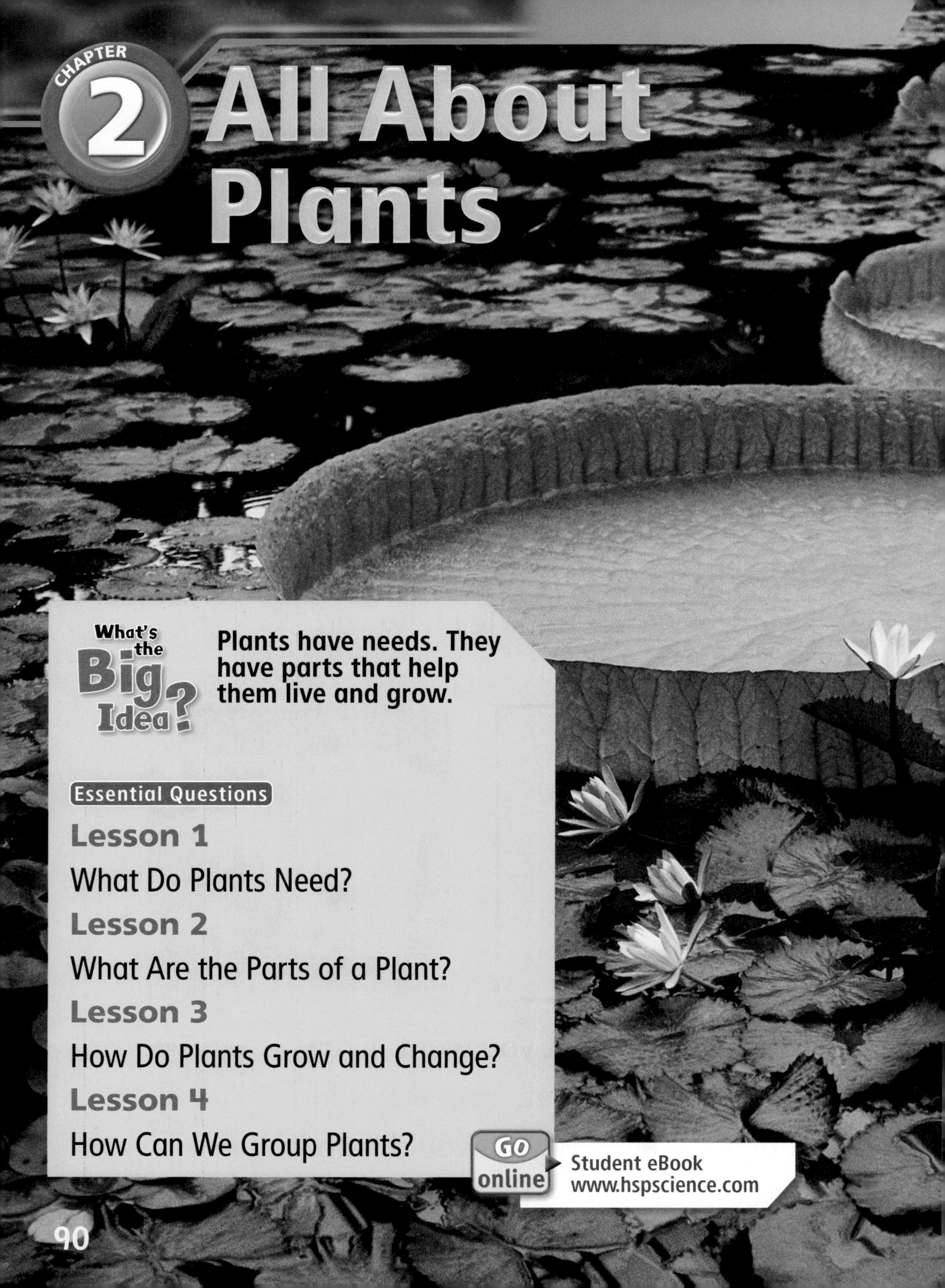

All About Plants

What's the Big Idea?

Plants have needs. They have parts that help them live and grow.

GO online

Student eBook
www.hspscience.com

How are these plants able to live in the water? How does this connect to the **Big Idea** for this chapter?

Victoria lilies

Investigate to find out the needs of plants.

Read and Learn about what plants need to live and stay healthy.

Essential Question

What Do Plants Need?

Fast Fact

Orchids
Orchids have roots that take water from the air. Predict what might happen if there were not enough water in the air.

orchids

Vocabulary Preview

sunlight p. 97

nutrients p. 98

93

Predict What Plants Need

Ask a Question

How would you take care of this plant?
Investigate to find out. Then read and learn to find out more.

Get Ready

Inquiry Skill Tip
When you predict, you use what you know to guess what will happen.

You need

index cards

2 small plants

spray
bottle

What to Do

Step ①

Label the plants. Put both plants in a sunny place.

Step ②

Water only one plant each day. **Predict** what will happen to each plant.

Step ③

After four days, check the plants. Did you **predict** correctly?

Draw Conclusions

What happened to the plant that did not get water?

Independent Inquiry

Take care of a young plant. **Predict** how tall it will be in two weeks. Was your prediction right?

VOCABULARY
sunlight
nutrients

Focus Skill **CAUSE AND EFFECT**
Look for all the things that
cause plants to grow.

Light, Air, and Water

A plant needs light, air, and water to
make its own food. The food helps the
plant grow and stay healthy. A plant
also needs water to move the food to all
its parts.

sunlight

air

96

water

Plants take in **sunlight**, or light from the sun. They take in water mostly from the soil.

Focus Skill **CAUSE AND EFFECT**

What would happen to a plant that did not have light, air, or water?

Make a Model Plant

Use paper, clay, craft sticks, and other art materials to make a model plant. Then tell about what a real plant needs to live.

Nutrients

Plants take in nutrients from the soil. **Nutrients** are minerals that plants use to grow.

 **CAUSE AND EFFECT**

Why does a plant need nutrients?

soil

Essential Question

What do plants need?

In this lesson, you learned that plants need sunlight, air, and water to live and grow.

1.  **CAUSE AND EFFECT** Make a chart like this one. Show what causes plants to grow.

cause → effect

2. VOCABULARY Use the words **sunlight** and **nutrients** to tell about this picture.

3. DRAW CONCLUSIONS What would happen if a plant did not get all the things it needs?

4. SUMMARIZE Use the chart to help you write a summary of the lesson. Tell about the needs of plants.

Test Prep

5. Why is soil important to plants?

Make Connections

 Writing

Write a Plan
You have a plant that does not look healthy. How could you make it healthy again? Write a plan. Tell what you would do. Draw a picture to show your plan.

I would give it water each day.

Investigate to find out the parts of a plant.

Read and Learn about the parts of plants and what they do to help plants live and grow.

Essential Question

What Are the Parts of a Plant?

Fast Fact

Elephant Ear Plant
Some leaves are so big that people can use them as umbrellas! You can communicate about the parts of a plant.

elephant ear plant

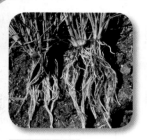

Parts of a Plant

Ask a Question

What are some parts of this fruit tree?
Investigate to find out. Then read and learn to find out more.

Get Ready

Inquiry Skill Tip

You can use pictures, numbers, or writing to communicate what you observe.

You need

hand lens

plant

crayons

What to Do

Step ①

Observe the parts of the plant. Use a hand lens.

Step ②

Draw what you see. Write about your picture.

Step ③

Share your work with a partner. **Communicate** what you observed.

Draw Conclusions

Did your partner's picture match yours? Explain.

Independent Inquiry

Put a white flower in colored water. Observe it for two days. **Communicate** what you observed.

Focus Skill **MAIN IDEA AND DETAILS**

Look for the parts of a plant and details about what the parts do.

Parts of a Plant

Plants have different parts. The parts help the plant live and grow. Most kinds of plants have roots, a stem, leaves, and flowers.

Focus Skill **MAIN IDEA AND DETAILS**

What are some parts of a plant?

flower

stem

leaf

roots

Roots

The **roots** hold the plant in the soil. They also take in the water and nutrients the plant needs.

 MAIN IDEA AND DETAILS

What are two ways roots help a plant?

How Roots Help

Push a craft stick deep into clay. Push another craft stick into clay just a little. Tap the side of each stick. What happens? How is the first stick like a plant with roots? How do roots hold a plant in place?

Where are the roots on these plants?

Stems

The **stem** holds up the plant. It carries food and water through the plant.

Stems may be green or woody. The trunks of trees are woody stems.

Focus Skill **MAIN IDEA AND DETAILS**

What are two ways the stem helps a plant?

Where are the stems on these plants?

106

Leaves

Leaves take in light and air. They need these things to make food for the plant. Different kinds of plants have leaves that look different. Leaves have different patterns.

MAIN IDEA AND DETAILS

What do leaves do?

What shapes and patterns do these leaves have?

Flowers, Fruits, and Seeds

Many plants have flowers. The **flowers** make fruits. The **fruits** hold seeds.

New plants may grow from the **seeds**. The new plants look like the plants that made the seeds.

Focus Skill MAIN IDEA AND DETAILS

What do flowers do?

seeds

flower

fruit

Essential Question

What are the parts of a plant?

In this lesson, you learned that plants have different parts that help them get what they need.

1. 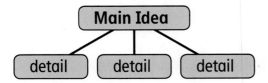 **MAIN IDEA AND DETAILS** Make a chart like this one. Show details of this main idea. **The parts of a plant help it live and grow.**

```
        Main Idea
    ┌──────┼──────┐
  detail  detail  detail
```

2. VOCABULARY Use the words **stem**, **leaves**, and **flowers** to tell about this picture.

3. DRAW CONCLUSIONS How do fruits help a plant?

4. SUMMARIZE Use the vocabulary words to write a lesson summary.

Test Prep

5. Which part of the plant makes food?

   A roots

   B leaves

   C flowers

   D fruits

Make Connections

123 Math

Measure Leaves
Put some leaves under a sheet of paper. Rub the leaves with unwrapped crayons. Measure the rubbings with small blocks. How many blocks long is each leaf?

Investigate to find out how seeds grow.

Read and Learn about the life cycles of plants.

How Do Plants Grow and Change?

Fast Fact

Coconuts

Coconuts come from coconut palms. They are the world's biggest seeds. You can sequence the parts of a plant's life.

Vocabulary Preview

seed coat p. 114

growing coconut palm

From Seed to Plant

Ask a Question

Observe the acorns. What kind of tree will these seeds become?

Investigate to find out. Then read and learn to find out more.

Get Ready

Inquiry Skill Tip

When you sequence things, you say what happened first, next, then, and last. You can draw pictures to show the order in which things happened.

You need

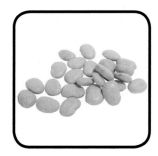

seeds

2 clear cups

colored cup

soil

What to Do

Step ①

Fill one clear cup with soil. Plant two seeds near the side. Water the seeds.

Step ②

Put the clear cup into the colored cup. Take it out each day, draw the seeds, and put it back.

Step ③

After three days, sequence your pictures to show what happened to the seeds.

Draw Conclusions

What happened to the seeds after three days?

Independent Inquiry

Observe a covered plant for four weeks. Draw a picture each week. Sequence your pictures.

VOCABULARY
seed coat

 **SEQUENCE**
Look for what happens first
next, then, and last as a seed
grows into a plant.

How Plants Grow

Most plants grow from seeds. Some
seeds have a seed coat. A **seed coat** is
a covering that protects the seed. Inside
the seed is a tiny plant. If the seed gets
water and warmth, the plant in it may
start to grow.

seed

seed coat

15 days

First, the roots grow down into the soil. Next, a stem grows up. Then, leaves and flowers grow. Last, the flowers make fruits that hold seeds. The seeds may grow into new plants.

Focus Skill SEQUENCE What happens after the flowers grow?

60 days

45 days

What's Inside?
Peel the seed coat off a bean seed. Then open the seed. Use a hand lens to observe what is inside. Can you find the tiny plant?

How Pine Trees Grow

Like other plants, most trees grow from seeds. Roots grow down. A green stem grows up. As it grows, the stem becomes woody. The stem of a tree is called a trunk.

This pine tree does not have flowers. It has cones. The cones hold seeds for new trees. Year after year, more branches and new cones grow. The trunk grows taller and thicker.

(Focus Skill) **SEQUENCE** **What happens to a tree year after year?**

cones

seed sprouting

seedling

adult tree

small tree

Seeds

Seeds may look different, but they are the same in an important way. They can grow into new plants. The new plant will look like the plant that made the seed.

Where are the seeds in these pictures?

peas

strawberry

sunflower

avocado

pepper

Essential Question

How do plants grow and change?

In this lesson, you learned how a seed grows into a plant.

1.  **SEQUENCE** Make a chart like this one. Show the life cycle of a tree.

☐ → ☐ → ☐

2. VOCABULARY Use the words **seed coat** to talk about this picture.

3. DRAW CONCLUSIONS What is the same about the ways trees and other plants grow? What is different?

4. SUMMARIZE Use the chart to help you write a lesson summary. Tell about how a seed grows into a plant.

Test Prep

5. What will the plant that grows from a seed be like? How do you know?

Make Connections

 Math

Compare Results

Copy the chart. Find out about more plants. Put them in order by how long they live, from shortest life to longest. Which live longer, trees or other plants?

How Long Some Plants Live	
beans	3 months
radishes	2 years

119

Investigate to find out how leaves can be classified.

Read and Learn about different groups of plants.

Essential Question

How Can We Group Plants?

Fast Fact

Kinds of Trees

There are many kinds of trees. Each tree has leaves that look different. You can classify plants by ways they are alike and different.

colorful leaves

edible p. 126

nonedible p. 127

Classify Leaves

Guided Inquiry

Ask a Question

Observe these leaves. How can you classify them? Investigate to find out. Then read and learn to find out more.

Get Ready

Inquiry Skill Tip

When you classify things, you group them by how they are alike. You can write, draw, or tell how you classify things.

You need

6 leaves   index cards

What to Do

Step ①

Compare the leaves. Do you see any patterns? **Classify** them into two groups.

Step ②

Use index cards to make labels for the groups.

Step ③

Tell how you classified your leaves.

Draw Conclusions

Why did you classify the leaves the way you did?

Independent Inquiry

Draw pictures of plants that are edible and nonedible. **Classify** them into groups.

COMPARE AND CONTRAST
Look for ways plants are alike
and different.

Grouping Plants

One way to group plants
is by looking at their parts.
Grasses are one kind of
plant. They all have long,
thin leaves. They also have
very small flowers. You often
do not see the flowers. They
get cut off when you cut the
grass.

grass

grass

Trees and shrubs are groups of plants. They both have woody stems. Most trees have one big main stem. Shrubs have many smaller stems. Some trees and shrubs may have flowers, too.

tree

COMPARE AND CONTRAST

How are these plants alike and different?

shrub

Plants You Can Eat

You can group plants by whether it is safe to eat them. **Edible** things are safe to eat. Some kinds of plants that have edible parts are tomatoes, onions, and squash.

What edible plants can you get at this market?

Plants you can not eat safely are **nonedible** plants.

 COMPARE AND CONTRAST
What is the difference between edible plants and nonedible plants?

Looking at Lunch
Observe your lunch. Draw a picture of it. Label the parts that come from plants. What are some kinds of plants you eat?

Ways We Use Plants

You can make groups of plants that people use to make things. People use cotton to make clothing and trees to make houses and toys.

★ Focus Skill **COMPARE AND CONTRAST**
How are cotton plants and trees alike?

cotton

cotton shirt

wooden toy

pine tree

Essential Question

How can we group plants?

In this lesson, you learned about ways we use plants and some ways they can be grouped.

1. ⭐ Focus Skill **COMPARE AND CONTRAST** Make a chart like this one. Use it to compare trees and shrubs.

alike ——— different

2. VOCABULARY Use the word **edible** to talk about this picture.

3. DRAW CONCLUSIONS What are some ways people use plants?

4. SUMMARIZE Write two sentences that summarize the lesson. Tell about the different groups of plants.

Test Prep

5. Which plant do many people use to make clothing?

A cotton   **B** grass
C pine tree   **D** shrub

Make Connections

 Social Studies

Plant Product Collage
Cut out pictures of things people get from plants. Make groups of food, clothing, and things from a home. Glue the pictures onto a sheet of paper.

George Washington Carver

▶ **GEORGE WASHINGTON CARVER**

▶ Plant Scientist

George Washington Carver was a plant scientist. Some people called him "the plant doctor." Carver worked with farmers who grew crops. He showed them how to plant peanuts to keep their soil healthy.

Carver thought of 300 things to make with peanut plants! Can you imagine washing your hair with shampoo made from peanuts? He also made foods, medicines, soaps, paints, rubber, gasoline, and paper—all from the peanut plant.

 Think and Write

Why is it important for farmers to keep their soil healthy?

Dr. Maria Elena Zavala

► **DR. MARIA ELENA ZAVALA**

► Plant Biologist

How do plants work? This is something Maria Elena Zavala wondered as a young girl. She took apart her father's roses to find out.

Plants were an important part of Maria Zavala's childhood. Her grandmother lived next door. She grew plants to use as medicine.

Today, Maria Zavala teaches at a university. She helps her students find out how plants work. She has won many awards for her work.

✏️ Think and Write

Why is it important to know how plants work?

Vocabulary Review

Look at the numbers next to the plant parts. Tell the number and the name of each part.

roots p. 105   flowers p. 108

stem p. 106   fruit p. 108

leaves p. 107   seeds p. 108

Check Understanding

7. What happens to a plant that gets air, light, water, and nutrients? Tell how you know.

8. You can eat corn. Which group does it belong in?

   A edible plants   **C** water

   B nonedible plants **D** trees

Critical Thinking

Over time, Hayden observes this tree in her back yard.

9. What is happening in each picture?

10. Predict what will happen to this tree next year. Tell how you know.

The Big Idea

Visual Summary

Tell how each picture shows the **Big Idea** for its chapter.

1 **Big Idea**

Animals are living things that have needs.

2 **Big Idea**

Plants have needs. They have parts that help them live and grow.

UNIT
B
LIFE SCIENCE

Living Together

Unit Inquiry

Animal Coverings
As you read this unit, you will see where plants and animals live. Plan and do a test. See how animals' coverings help animals live where they do.

CHAPTER 3 Environments for Living Things

What's the Big Idea?

Living things have special parts or behaviors that help them survive in their environments. Plants and animals need each other.

Essential Questions

Lesson 1

What Is an Environment?

Lesson 2

What Helps Plants and Animals Live in Places?

Lesson 3

How Do Plants and Animals Need Each Other?

Go online
Student eBook
www.hspscience.com

136

walking sticks

What do YOU wonder?

How are these insects able to hide in the plants? How does this help explain the Big Idea for this chapter?

137

Investigate to find out where some kinds of animals live.

Read and Learn about the living and nonliving things found in an environment and how people change their environment.

Essential Question

What Is an Environment?

Fast Fact

Jaguar's Home
Few people have ever seen jaguars in the wild. They live where it is easy to hide. Communicate what you know about where animals live.

138

environment
p. 142

jaguar on a branch

Where Animals Live

Guided Inquiry

Ask a Question

Where do these animals live? Investigate to find out. Then read and learn to find out more.

Get Ready

Inquiry Skill Tip

You can use pictures, numbers, or writing to communicate what you observe.

You need

crayons

animal picture cards

What to Do

Step 1

Look at the cards.
Choose an animal you
know about.

Step 2

Draw the animal where
it lives.

Step 3

Communicate with
classmates about what
you drew.

Draw Conclusions

How was your picture
different from your
classmates' pictures?
Explain.

Independent Inquiry

Observe your
environment at home.
Communicate with
a partner what you
observed.

MAIN IDEA AND DETAILS
Look for the main ideas about environments.

Environments

An **environment** is made up of all the things in a place.

An environment has living things. It has plants and animals.

Find living and nonliving things in this environment.

An environment also has nonliving things, such as rocks and water.

★ Focus Skill **MAIN IDEA AND DETAILS**
What is an environment?

Environments Near You

Go on a nature walk with your class. Observe the environment. What living things do you see? What nonliving things do you see? Make two lists.

People and Environments

People can change environments. They may build houses and roads. They may make new things. People made many of the things you see in your environment.

Focus Skill MAIN IDEA AND DETAILS

How can people change environments?

Which things here did people make? Which things were not made by people?

What is an environment?

In this lesson, you learned about the living and nonliving things in an environment and how environments can change.

1. 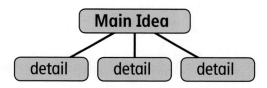 **MAIN IDEA AND DETAILS**
Make a chart like this one. Show the details of this main idea. **An environment is all of the things in a place.**

```
          Main Idea
      ┌───────┼───────┐
   detail   detail   detail
```

2. VOCABULARY
Tell about this animal's **environment**.

3. DRAW CONCLUSIONS
What are some living and nonliving things that can be found in an environment?

4. SUMMARIZE Write two sentences about the lesson. Use the word **environment**.

Test Prep
5. Tell about some ways people can change their environments.

Make Connections

 Writing

Write a Description
Look at the environment outside your school. Write sentences about things you see that were made by people. Tell what each thing looks like. Tell what it is used for.

The slide was made by people. It is red and blue. It is for kids to play on.

Essential Question

What Helps Plants and Animals Live in Places?

Investigate to find out how animals can hide in their environments.

Read and Learn about plant and animal adaptations.

Fast Fact

Alligator Adaptation

An alligator has eyes on the top of its head. Draw a conclusion about how this might help an alligator.

adaptation
p. 150

camouflage
p. 154

alligator

Some Animals Hide

Ask a Question

How are the color and shape of this animal helping it hide?
Investigate to find out. Then read and learn to find out more.

Get Ready

Inquiry Skill Tip

To draw a conclusion, use what you observe and what you already know to decide what something means.

You need

colored chips

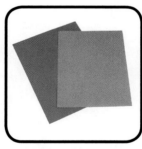

colored paper

What to Do

Step ①

Put the chips on a sheet of colored paper. Which chips are hard to see?

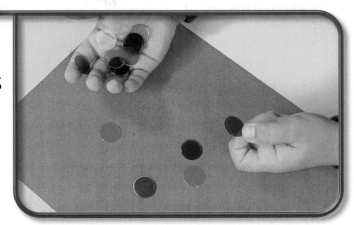

Step ②

Put the chips on a sheet of paper of a different color. Which chips are hard to see now?

Step ③

Draw a conclusion about how color helps some animals hide.

Draw Conclusions

Why was it easier to see the chips that were not the same color as the paper? Explain.

Independent Inquiry

Think about what living things need. **Draw a conclusion** about what body parts help you get the things you need.

VOCABULARY
adaptation
camouflage

Focus Skill COMPARE AND CONTRAST
Look for ways adaptations are alike and different.

Plant Adaptations

An **adaptation** is a body part or a behavior that helps a living thing.

Plants have adaptations. Some adaptations help them get water. A banyan tree has many roots. A jade plant has thick leaves that store water.

banyan tree

jade plant

150

Some adaptations help plants stay alive. Thorns on plants stop animals from eating them. Other adaptations help plants make new plants. Wings on maple fruits carry the seeds to new places. Flowers attract small animals. The animals help the plants make seeds.

Focus Skill **COMPARE AND CONTRAST** **What are some plant adaptations? How are they alike and different?**

maple seeds

rose

hummingbird

Animal Adaptations

Animals have adaptations, too. Some adaptations help animals eat. Sharp teeth help a lion bite meat. A long tongue helps an anteater get ants.

Some adaptations help animals move. Wings and feathers help a bird fly. Fins help a fish swim.

scarlet ibis

lion

anteater

Some adaptations keep animals safe. A porcupine has sharp quills. Other animals keep away from the quills.

 COMPARE AND CONTRAST
How are some animal adaptations alike?

Observe Beaks
Put crumbs from lunch on a tray. Put the tray outside where you can see it. Then watch for birds. What birds do you see? How does each one use its beak to eat?

goldfish

porcupine

153

Camouflage

Some animals have an adaptation called camouflage. **Camouflage** is a color or pattern that helps an animal hide. Animals need to hide to stay safe or to find food.

arctic fox in winter

arctic fox in summer

flounder

dead-leaf butterfly

frog

For more links and animations, go to **www.hspscience.com**

What helps plants and animals live in places?

In this lesson, you learned that plants and animals have adaptations that help them live in their environments.

1. (Focus Skill) **COMPARE AND CONTRAST**
Make a chart like this one. Use it to compare adaptations.

alike ———— different

2. VOCABULARY Use the word **adaptation** to tell about this picture.

3. DRAW CONCLUSIONS Why do you think some animals have camouflage?

4. SUMMARIZE Use the chart to help you summarize. Tell how adaptations help plants and animals.

Test Prep

5. Which adaptation helps plants store water?
   A flowers
   B sharp teeth
   C thick leaves
   D thorns

Make Connections

 **Math**

Counting Teeth

Some animals have many teeth. Others do not. How many teeth do you have? Use a mirror to count. Use the data to make a class graph. Does everyone have the same number of teeth?

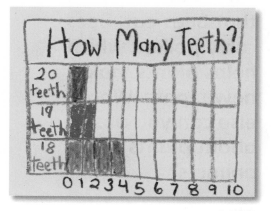

155

Investigate to find out how animals use trees.

Read and Learn about how plants and animals help each other.

Essential Question

How Do Plants and Animals Need Each Other?

Fast Fact

Bees Helping Plants

Flowers make food that bees eat. Bees carry pollen, which helps plants make new plants. What else can you observe about plants and animals?

156

What to Do

Step ①

Find a tree with your class. Observe it with a hand lens. Record what you see.

Step ②

Sit quietly and observe. Record what animals in your tree are doing.

Step ③

How did animals use the tree? Talk about what you observed.

Draw Conclusions

How did the tree help the animals get what they needed?

Independent Inquiry

Observe ways people use plants. How is wood used in your classroom? Make a list.

VOCABULARY
oxygen
pollen
food chain

 MAIN IDEA AND DETAILS
Look for the main ideas about how animals use plants and help plants.

Animals Use Plants

Animals use plants to meet their needs. Some live in plants or use them to make homes. Plants are good places for animals to hide in, too.

heron hiding in grass

deer hiding behind trees

beaver building a dam

Some animals use plants for food. Animals need to breathe oxygen from the air. **Oxygen** is a kind of gas. Plants put oxygen into the air.

⭐ Focus Skill MAIN IDEA AND DETAILS

What are three ways animals use plants?

Homes from Plants

Some birds use plant parts and mud to make nests. Use twigs, grass, and clay to make a model of a bird's nest.

elephants eating leaves

Animals Help Plants

Some animals help plants make new plants. They carry **pollen** from flower to flower. Pollen is a powder that flowers need to make seeds.

honey possum carrying pollen

butterfly carrying pollen

Some animals help plants by carrying seeds. They take seeds to new places. The seeds may grow into new plants there.

⭐ **Focus Skill** **MAIN IDEA AND DETAILS**

How can animals help plants make new plants?

squirrel carrying seeds

dog carrying seeds

Food Chain

Animals can be grouped by what they eat. Some animals eat plants. Some eat other animals. A **food chain** shows how animals and plants are linked.

(Focus Skill) **MAIN IDEA AND DETAILS**

What does a food chain show?

Last, a bear eats the fish.

Next, a rainbow trout eats the stonefly.

First, a stonefly eats part of a plant.

Essential Question

How do plants and animals need each other?

In this lesson, you learned that animals help plants. You also learned that plants help animals.

1. 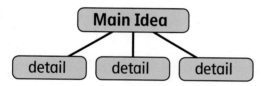 **MAIN IDEA AND DETAILS**
Make a chart like this one. Show details of this main idea. **Animals and plants need each other.**

Main Idea

detail detail detail

2. VOCABULARY

Use the word **pollen** to tell about this picture.

3. DRAW CONCLUSIONS How do plants help animals?

4. SUMMARIZE Use the vocabulary words to write a summary of the lesson.

Test Prep

5. Which of these shows how animals are linked?

A air
B environment
C flowers
D food chain

Make Connections

 Social Studies

You Need Plants and Animals
How do you use plants and animals to meet your needs? Draw pictures and write sentences to show the ways. Put your pages together to make a book.

Steve Irwin

Most children do not learn how to jump into a river and catch crocodiles at the age of nine. Steve Irwin did. His parents owned a reptile park. Taking care of crocodiles, snakes, and other animals was just part of their family life.

Steve Irwin grew to love all kinds of animals. He shared this love in his television shows *The Crocodile Hunter* and *Croc Files*. He talked a lot about saving animals in the wild. Many visitors have come to his family's animal park, now called Australia Zoo. At the zoo, he taught people all about animals and how he helped them.

▶ **STEVE IRWIN**
▶ Wildlife Expert

✏️ Think and Write

Steve Irwin called himself and others like him "Wildlife Warriors." What do you think that means?

Salim Ali

▶ **SALIM ALI**

▶ Ornithologist

Who was nicknamed "The Birdman of India?" That was Salim Ali. He was a famous ornithologist. An ornithologist is a scientist who studies birds.

As a young child, Salim was curious about some birds with yellow throats. He went to the Bombay Natural History Society to find out more. There, his love of birds began.

Salim Ali learned all he could about birds. Then he began a project. He explored parts of India and studied the birds he found there. He wrote several books about his findings. Today, people who study birds learn a great deal from his work.

 Think and Write

Salim Ali discovered some rare kinds of birds and wrote about them. Why is this important?

Vocabulary Review

Choose the best word to complete each sentence.

environment p. 142   **oxygen** p. 161

camouflage p. 154   **pollen** p. 162

1. Powder from flowers is _____.

2. A gas that is part of air is _____.

3. An adaptation that helps an animal hide is _____.

4. A place that is made up of living and nonliving things is an _____.

Check Understanding

5. Name two animals. Tell how the adaptations of these animals are **alike**. Then tell how they are **different**.

Focus Skill

6. How do plants help animals breathe?

    A Plants put oxygen into the air.

    B Animals eat plants.

    C Plants store water.

    D Animals can hide in plants.

Critical Thinking

7. What is an adaptation? Name three plant adaptations. Tell how each adaptation helps a plant survive in its environment.

The Big Idea

8. Look at these plants and animals. Draw them in order to show a food chain. Write about what happens.

Places to Live

What's the Big Idea?

Forests, deserts, and oceans are different habitats. Plants and animals have special parts that help them live in these places.

Essential Questions

GO online ▶ Student eBook
www.hspscience.com

clown fish and
sea anemones

What do **YOU** wonder?

Why do these fish live
here? How does that help
explain the **Big Idea** for
this chapter?

Essential Question

What Lives in a Forest?

Investigate to find out the kinds of bark and leaves different trees have.

Read and Learn about the plants and animals that live in a forest.

Fast Fact

Redwood Forest
The trees in this redwood forest are the world's tallest living things. You can compare trees by size.

forest p. 176

habitat p. 178

Redwood bark has deep grooves.

173

Compare Leaves and Bark

Guided Inquiry

Ask a Question

What kind of bark and leaves do you think these trees have?
Investigate to find out. Then read and learn to find out more.

Get Ready

Inquiry Skill Tip

When you compare, you look for ways things are alike and different. You can draw pictures to show how you compared the objects.

You need

dark-colored crayon

paper

What to Do

Step ❶

Go outside with your class. Find a leaf. Make a rubbing.

Step ❷

Find the tree that the leaf is from. Make a rubbing of its bark.

Step ❸

Compare your rubbings with a classmate's rubbings. Tell what you see.

Draw Conclusions

How are your rubbings different from your classmate's rubbings?

Independent Inquiry

Go on a leaf hunt with your class. Draw a picture of four different leaves. **Compare** your drawings.

VOCABULARY
forest
habitat

MAIN IDEA AND DETAILS
Look for the main ideas about forests.

Forests

A **forest** is land that is covered with trees. The trees shade the forest floor. The shade helps the soil stay moist.

MAIN IDEA AND DETAILS What is a forest?

Forest Plants

In a forest, trees get enough rain and warmth to grow tall. Their leaves can get the light they need. Ferns and flowers grow on the forest floor. They need water, but they do not need much light.

ferns

 MAIN IDEA AND DETAILS

How do trees get the light they need?

wildflowers

Made in the Shade

Wet two paper towels. Put them in a sunny place. Use a folder to make shade for one towel. Wait a few minutes. Then check the towels. Which one is wetter? How is the wetter towel like a forest floor?

177

Forest Animals

A forest has habitats for many animals. A **habitat** is a place where an animal finds food, water, and shelter. A bear needs a large part of a forest for its habitat. A smaller animal may need only a log.

(Focus Skill) MAIN IDEA AND DETAILS

What are some animals that may have habitats in a forest?

eagle

bear

skunk

How are these animals meeting their needs?

What lives in a forest?

In this lesson, you learned about some of the plants and animals that live in a forest.

1. **Focus Skill MAIN IDEA AND DETAILS**
Make a chart like this one. Show details for this main idea. **A forest is a place where many trees grow.**

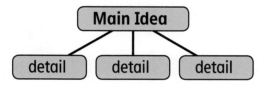

Main Idea

detail   detail   detail

2. VOCABULARY
Use the words **forest** and **habitat** to tell about this picture.

3. DRAW CONCLUSIONS How do ferns and flowers get the water they need?

4. SUMMARIZE Use the chart to help you write a summary. Tell about forest plants and animals.

Test Prep
5. Why could a log be a good habitat for a small animal?

Make Connections

 Writing

Write a Story
Write a story about a forest animal. Tell where it lives, what it eats, and what it does. Draw pictures that show the animal in the forest.

This bear lives in the forest with her mom and her brother.

Investigate to find out how some plants can live in the desert.

Read and Learn about some kinds of plants and animals that live in the desert.

Essential Question

What Lives in a Desert?

Fast Fact

Desert Plants
A barrel cactus can live for almost 6 years on water stored in its stem. You can draw a conclusion about why some plants can live in deserts.

desert p. 184

barrel cactus with yellow fruit

Desert Plants

Guided Inquiry

Ask a Question

What parts do you think help the tree live in the desert? Investigate to find out. Then read and learn to find out more.

Get Ready

Inquiry Skill Tip

To draw a conclusion, use what you observe and what you already know to decide what something means.

You need

2 paper-towel leaf shapes

water

wax paper

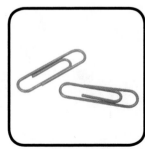

2 paper clips

What to Do

Step ①

Make the leaf shapes damp. Fold the wax paper. Put one leaf inside the fold. Clip it.

Step ②

Put the leaf shapes in a sunny place. Observe them in one hour.

Step ③

Which leaf was still damp? Why? Draw a conclusion.

Draw Conclusions

How can a waxy covering help a plant live in the desert?

Independent Inquiry

Observe a cactus with a hand lens. Draw a conclusion about how parts of a cactus help it stay safe.

VOCABULARY
desert

 **MAIN IDEA AND DETAILS**
Look for the main ideas about deserts.

Deserts

A **desert** is land that gets very little rain. Most deserts are sunny all year long. The soil is very dry. Only some kinds of plants and animals can live there.

creosote

 **MAIN IDEA AND DETAILS** **How can you tell if a place is a desert?**

Desert Plants

Desert plants do not need much water. A cactus is a desert plant. It can hold water in its thick stem. Its waxy covering helps keep water in.

Focus Skill **MAIN IDEA AND DETAILS** How does a cactus live without much water?

brittlebush

Insta-Lab

Soak It Up

Get a sponge that is very dry. Put water on it a little at a time. Observe the sponge. How does it change? How is the sponge like the stem of a cactus?

Desert Animals

Desert animals need to keep cool and find water. The dove and the hare rest in shady places. The tortoise gets water from its food.

 MAIN IDEA AND DETAILS

What are important needs of desert animals?

desert hare

white-winged dove

How are these animals meeting their needs?

desert tortoise

What lives in a desert?

In this lesson, you learned about some kinds of plants and animals that live in a desert.

1. 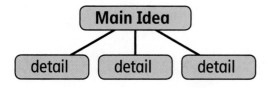 **MAIN IDEA AND DETAILS**
Make a chart like this one. Show details of this main idea. **A desert is land that gets very little rain.**

2. VOCABULARY Use the word **desert** to tell about this picture.

3. DRAW CONCLUSIONS Why are few plants and animals able to live in a desert?

4. SUMMARIZE Use the chart to write a summary of the lesson. Tell about desert plants and animals.

Test Prep

5. Which word best describes a desert?

   A cloudy

   B cool

   C dry

   D wet

Make Connections

123 Math

Measure Rainfall
Deserts get less than 25 centimeters of rain each year. How much rain falls where you live? Measure that amount and 25 centimeters on a sheet of paper. Compare.

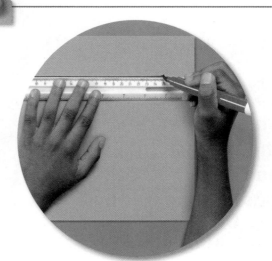

Investigate to find out how animals in the ocean are alike and different.

Read and Learn about some kinds of animals that live in the ocean.

What Lives in an Ocean?

Fast Fact

Ocean Animals
Blue whales are the biggest animals on Earth. You can classify animals by size.

blue whale mother
and young

ocean p. 192

Animals in the Ocean

Ask a Question

How can you classify these animals?
Investigate to find out. Then read and learn to find out more.

Get Ready

Inquiry Skill Tip

When you classify things, you group them by how they are alike. You can tell others how you classify things.

You need

ocean animal picture cards

What to Do

Step 1

Observe the animals. How are they alike? How are they different?

Step 2

Classify the animals into groups.

Step 3

Tell how the animals in each group are alike. Tell how the two groups are different.

Draw Conclusions

What are some ways ocean animals are different from each other?

Independent Inquiry

Where do ocean animals live? Get some books from the library. **Classify** animals by where they live.

VOCABULARY
ocean

 MAIN IDEA AND DETAILS
Look for the main ideas about oceans.

Oceans

An **ocean** is a large body of salt water. Oceans cover much of Earth.

Ocean animals live where they can find food. Crabs find their food near the shore.

goatfish

hermit crab

192

Essential Question

What lives in an ocean?

In this lesson, you learned about some of the animals that live in the ocean and how they find food.

1. 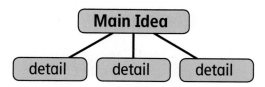 **MAIN IDEA AND DETAILS**
Make a chart like this one. Show details of this main idea. **Ocean animals live where they can find food.**

```
        Main Idea
      /     |     \
  detail  detail  detail
```

2. VOCABULARY
Use the word **ocean** to tell about this picture.

3. DRAW CONCLUSIONS
Where do ocean animals find food?

4. SUMMARIZE Write two sentences that summarize the lesson. Tell about oceans.

Test Prep
5. Why do many animals live on coral reefs?

Make Connections

 Social Studies

Oceans of the World
Look at a globe or a map that shows all of Earth. Write down the names of the oceans you see. What do you observe about the oceans? What other bodies of water do you see?

195

A New Plane Fights Fires

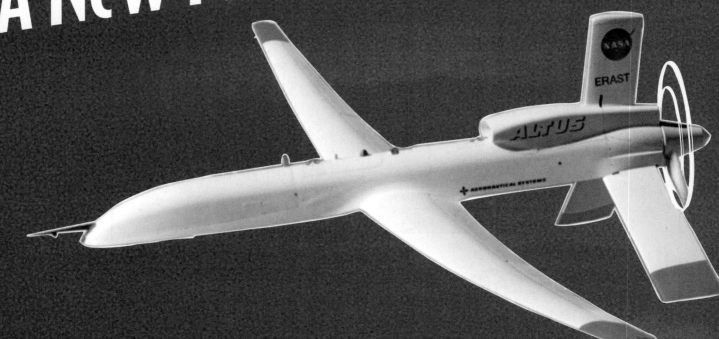

Wildfires burn large parts of forests in the western United States. Wildfires can move quickly. This can put firefighters in danger.

Now firefighters have a new tool to help them. This tool is a robot plane called Altus II.

Plane Without a Pilot

Altus II is 17 meters (55 feet) across. It can fly at about 185 kilometers (115 miles) per hour. The plane does not have a pilot. It is controlled by people on the ground.

Altus II has cameras on board. It takes pictures of fires. The cameras can see through smoke. They can also see places that might catch fire.

The plane can also be used by people to keep track of floods or hurricanes.

✍ Think and Write

How does using Altus II help firefighters?

All in a Day's Work

Altus II is light. It does not need much fuel. It can fly for up to 24 hours at a time.

Find out more. Log on to www.hspscience.com

Vocabulary Review

Use the words below to complete the sentences.

forest p. 176   **desert** p. 184

habitat p. 178   **ocean** p. 192

1. A large body of salt water is called an _____.

2. A place where an animal can find food, water, and shelter is a _____.

3. Land that is covered with trees is a _____.

4. Land that gets little rain is a _____.

Check Understanding

5. **Compare** these animals' habitats.

6. Why is a coral reef a good habitat for this eel?

  A A coral reef is very dry.

  B The eel can live without much water.

  C The eel needs shade.

  D The eel can find food and shelter.

Critical Thinking

7. Read the clues in the sentences below. Name the plant. Tell where it lives.

This plant needs rain and warmth to grow. It grows tall so that its leaves can get light.

8. Write clues about a plant or animal from this chapter. Ask a partner to name your plant or animal.

Tell how each picture shows the **Big Idea** for its chapter.

CHAPTER 3 Big Idea

Living things have special parts or behaviors that help them survive in their environments. Plants and animals need each other.

CHAPTER 4 Big Idea

Forests, deserts, and oceans are different habitats. Plants and animals have special parts that help them live in these places.

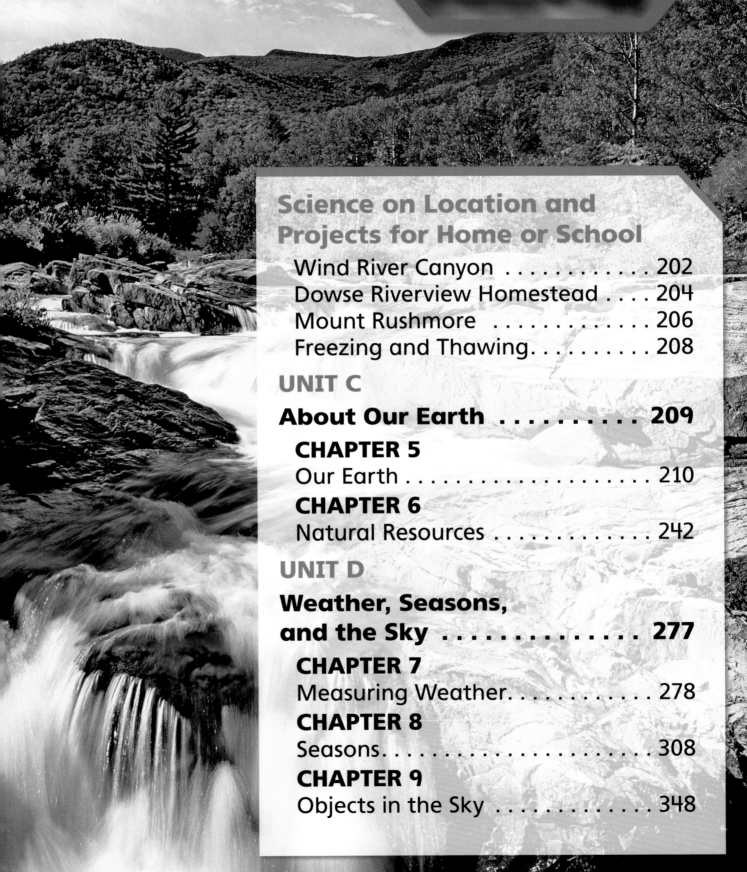

EARTH SCIENCE

Wind River Canyon

Do you wonder how Earth changes? Do you wonder what forces change Earth? Wind River Canyon shows how moving water can change land. The canyon is in Wyoming. The Wind River flows through it.

water changing the land

How Wind River Canyon Formed

The Wind River carved the canyon, but other forces helped. At times, Earth's crust lifted. Weather wore away the rock. Streams and rivers flowed over the land. Water carried away rocks and soil. In some places, rivers cut downward. This is what the Wind River did. It carved the canyon. This took millions of years. Wind River Canyon has some of Earth's oldest rocks.

Think And Write

❶ **Scientific Thinking** What is a canyon?

❷ **Scientific Thinking** What does Wind River Canyon tell you about Earth?

Wind River

The Dowse Riverview Homestead

Many settlers in Nebraska built sod houses.

Do you know what sod is? It is a strip of soil with grass and roots growing in it. William Dowse used sod "bricks" to build his house in 1900. The Dowse Sod House still stands today. It is in Custer County, Nebraska.

sod bricks

Building a Sod House

The first step in building a sod house was to find a field with grass that had thick roots. Roots held the soil together. Next, the settler used a special plow to cut the sod into long strips. Then the settler cut the strips into "bricks" and used the bricks to make the walls. The walls were more than two feet thick. This helped keep the house warm in winter and cool in summer. Sod houses had windows and doors. Wood was used to frame them. Sod roofs leaked, so settlers had to find other materials to use.

Think And Write

1. **Scientific Inquiry** What is a sod house?

2. **Science and Technology** How is a sod house like your home? How is it different? Use pictures and words to explain your ideas.

Mount Rushmore

Mount Rushmore is in the Black Hills of South Dakota. Do you see the four stone faces? They are the faces of Presidents. Can you name them? People carved the faces in the side of the mountain. They are carved from granite. Granite is one kind of rock. It is very hard. It is often used to make important buildings.

Mount Rushmore

Carving Mount Rushmore

Mount Rushmore is the work of Gutzon Borglum. He was a sculptor. He and 400 other workers carved the faces. Each day, they had to climb 506 steps to get to the top of the mountain. The workers used drills, jackhammers, and wedges. They used dynamite to blast away tons of rock. They began in 1927. The work took 14 years.

Each face is 60 feet high.

Think And Write

1. **Science and Technology** Why did the workers have to use tools such as drills and jackhammers to carve the faces?

2. **Scientific Thinking** How is granite used?

Project   Freezing and Thawing

You need
- plastic wrap
- water
- modeling clay
- freezer

What to Do

❶ Wet some modeling clay with water. Make two "rocks" about the same size.

❷ Wrap each one in plastic wrap.

❸ Put one rock in the freezer for at least 24 hours.

❹ Unwrap the two rocks. Compare.

Draw Conclusions

❶ What happened to the rock you froze? What might happen if you thawed it, wet it, and froze it?

❷ What might happen after many weeks to real rocks that freeze at night and thaw during the day?

Design Your Own Investigation

Soil Sample Shake

What things can be found in soil? Get some soil, water, and a jar. Plan an investigation to answer the question. Record what you observe. Share your results with your classmates.

About Our Earth

Unit Inquiry

Plants and Soil

As you read this unit, you will find out about Earth's soil. Plan and do a test. See if plants change the amount of soil that is washed away by water.

CHAPTER 5 Our Earth

 **What's the Big Idea?**

Earth has landforms and bodies of water. Water can change Earth.

Essential Questions

Lesson 1

What Are Some Kinds of Land?

Lesson 2

What Are Some Kinds of Water?

Lesson 3

How Does Earth Change?

GO ► Student eBook

Niagara Falls

What do YOU wonder?

How have the river and waterfall changed Earth over time? How does this help explain the Big Idea for this chapter?

Essential Question

What Are Some Kinds of Land?

Investigate to find out how kinds of land are alike and different.

Read and Learn about some different kinds of landforms on Earth.

Fast Fact

Mount McKinley
Mt. McKinley, in Alaska, is our country's highest mountain. You can classify land by height, shape, and where it is.

snow on Mount McKinley

Kinds of Land

Ask a Question

What kind of land is this? How do you know?
Investigate to find out. Then read and learn to find out more.

Get Ready

Inquiry Skill Tip

When you classify things, you group them by how they are alike. You can tell about how you classify things.

You need

land picture cards

What to Do

Step ①

Look at the pictures. Tell how they are alike and how they are different.

Step ②

Classify the picture cards. Group pictures by the kinds of land they show.

Step ③

Talk about the groups you made.

Draw Conclusions

How did you classify the pictures of the landforms?

Independent Inquiry

Look through old magazines. Cut out pictures of landforms. Classify the pictures.

VOCABULARY

hill   beach
valley

 COMPARE AND CONTRAST

Read to find out how kinds of land can be alike and different.

Mountains and Hills

Land on Earth has different shapes. One land shape is a mountain. A **mountain** is the highest kind of land. It has sides that slope up to a top. Some mountains have rocky peaks. Others are round on top.

mountain

A **hill** is a high place that is smaller than a mountain. Most hills are round on top.

 **COMPARE AND CONTRAST**

How are mountains and hills alike?

hills

217

Valleys and Plains

Valleys and plains are lower lands. A **valley** is low land between mountains or hills. A **plain** is flat land that spreads out a long way.

 **COMPARE AND CONTRAST**

How are valleys and plains different?

valley

plain

Insta-Lab

Model Land

Use clay or damp sand to model kinds of land. Work with a partner. Show a mountain, a hill, a valley, and a plain. Label each land shape.

219

Beaches

In some places, a lake or an ocean has a beach. A **beach** is flat, sandy land along a shore. Some beaches can also be rocky.

Focus Skill **COMPARE AND CONTRAST** How is a beach different from other kinds of land?

beach

Essential Question

What are some kinds of land?

In this lesson, you learned about how mountains, hills, valleys, plains, and beaches are alike and different.

1. **Focus Skill** **COMPARE AND CONTRAST**
Make a chart like this one. Use it to compare Earth's landforms.

alike — different

2. VOCABULARY Write a sentence to tell how **plains** and **mountains** are different.

3. DRAW CONCLUSIONS
How are plains and beaches alike? How are they different?

4. SUMMARIZE Use the vocabulary words to write a summary of the lesson.

Test Prep
5. Which of these is flat, sandy land along a shore?
   A beach
   B hill
   C mountain
   D valley

Make Connections

 Writing

Essay
Choose a kind of land you would like to visit. Write about why you want to go and what you would do there. Then draw a picture of yourself in that place.

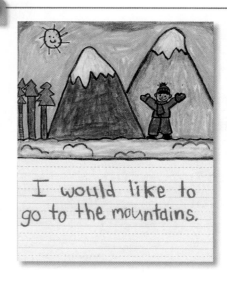

I would like to go to the mountains.

221

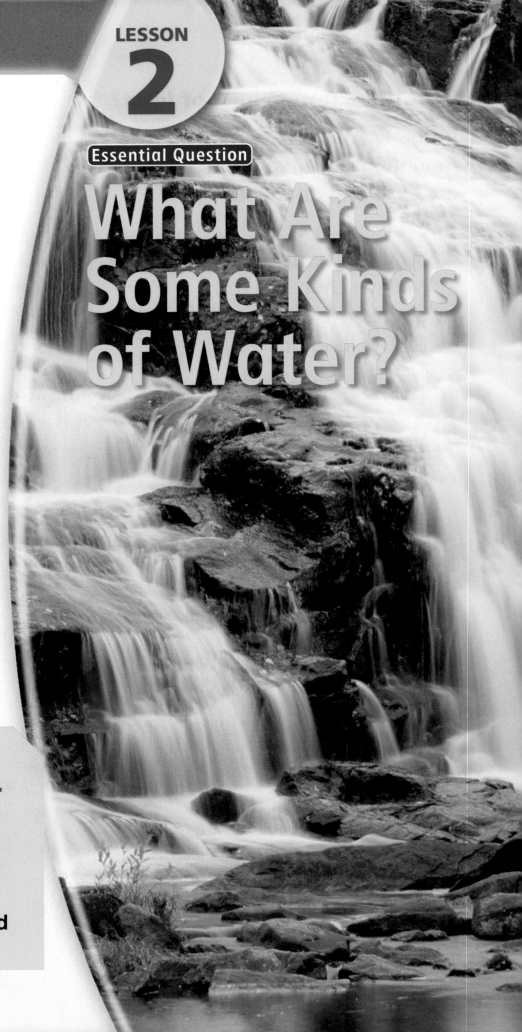

Investigate to find out how Earth's land and water are different.

Read and Learn about the kinds of water on Earth.

Essential Question

What Are Some Kinds of Water?

Fast Fact

Flowing Water
This river has been flowing over these rocks for thousands of years. You can infer how water and land are different.

stream p. 226

river p. 226

lake p. 227

ocean p. 228

waterfall

Explore Land and Water

Ask a Question

Which parts of the picture show land? Which parts show water?

Investigate to find out. Then read and learn to find out more.

Get Ready

Inquiry Skill Tip

When you infer, you use what you observed to tell why something happened.

You need

globe

What to Do

Step ①

Observe the globe.
What can you see?

Step ②

Find land. Then find water.
How do you know the
difference?

Step ③

Infer how Earth's land and
water are different.

Draw Conclusions

How does the globe show
the difference between
land and water?

Independent Inquiry

Observe a globe. Find
blue shapes. **Infer** how
the shapes show different
kinds of water.

COMPARE AND CONTRAST
Look for ways bodies of water are alike and ways they are different.

Streams, Rivers, and Lakes

Streams, rivers, and lakes are bodies of fresh water. A **stream** is a small body of moving water. Streams may begin in mountains. The water flows downhill. The streams flow together into a river. A **river** is a large body of moving water.

stream

river

lake

Rivers flow together. Rivers may flow into lakes and oceans. A **lake** is a still body of water with land around most of it.

★ Focus Skill **COMPARE AND CONTRAST**

How are rivers and streams alike?

Insta-Lab

Moving Water

Cut a cardboard tube in half the long way. Put the halves on a tray. Put something under one end of one half. Pour water into each half. Observe. Infer how the land's shape makes rivers flow quickly or slowly.

Oceans

An **ocean** is a large body of salty water. Most of Earth's water is in oceans.

⭐ **COMPARE AND CONTRAST**

How are oceans different from other bodies of water?

ocean

Essential Question

What are some kinds of water?

In this lesson, you learned about streams, rivers, lakes, and oceans.

1.  **COMPARE AND CONTRAST** Make a chart like this one. Use it to compare Earth's bodies of water.

alike ——— different

2. VOCABULARY Tell how you know this is a **river**.

3. DRAW CONCLUSIONS Tell whether a river will flow faster down a steep hill or a gentle hill.

4. SUMMARIZE Use the vocabulary words to write a summary of the lesson.

Test Prep

5. How are streams, rivers, and lakes alike?

Make Connections

123 Math

Model Fractions

Draw a circle. Divide it into 4 equal parts. Color 3 parts blue and 1 part brown. What does this show about the water and land on Earth? Write the fraction.

Investigate to find out how water changes mountains.

Read and Learn about how weather and moving water can change Earth.

Essential Question

How Does Earth Change?

Fast Fact

Hoodoos
Water and wind change the shape of these rocks a little each year. You can make models to learn how water changes Earth.

flood p. 234

drought p. 235

erosion p. 236

hoodoos in Bryce Canyon

231

Model Erosion

Guided Inquiry

Ask a Question

How have these rocks changed over time? Investigate to find out. Then read and learn to find out more.

Get Ready

Inquiry Skill Tip

Some changes take a long time. You can make a model to see how the changes happen.

You need

damp soil

tray

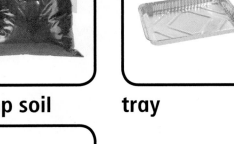

water

232

What to Do

Step ❶

Use soil to **make a model** of a mountain.

Step ❷

Slowly pour water onto the top of the mountain.

Step ❸

Observe. How does the mountain change? Tell how the **model** shows how water changes real mountains.

Draw Conclusions

How does the model show how water changes a mountain over time?

Independent Inquiry

Find out how water can change a rock. **Make a model** using chalk to find out what happens.

VOCABULARY
flood
drought
erosion

CAUSE AND EFFECT

Look for ways that water can change Earth.

Weather Changes Earth

Heavy rains may cause a flood. A **flood** happens when rivers and streams get too full. The water flows onto land. A flood may carry soil to a new place.

flood

This is the same place during a drought.

Dry weather may cause a drought. A **drought** is a long time with less rain than usual. The land gets very dry. Plants may die.

Focus Skill CAUSE AND EFFECT

What can weather do to Earth's land?

Insta-Lab

Flooding

Fill two trays with dry soil. Slowly pour 1 cup of water onto one tray. Then quickly pour 1 cup of water onto the other tray. What happens? Infer why some rains cause floods and others do not.

The Grand Canyon

Moving water changes the land. It carries rocks and soil to new places. This is called **erosion**. Erosion formed the Grand Canyon over millions of years.

1. **A long time ago, water began to flow over the land.**

2. **The moving water carried away soil and rocks.**

3. **The water's path became very deep. In time, it formed the Grand Canyon.**

For more links and animations, go to **www.hspscience.com**

Essential Question

How does Earth change?

In this lesson, you learned about how Earth is changed by floods, droughts, and erosion.

1.  **CAUSE AND EFFECT**
Make a chart like this one. Show what causes some changes to Earth.

cause ➔ effect

2. VOCABULARY
Use the word **erosion** to talk about this picture.

3. DRAW CONCLUSIONS
What happens in a drought?

4. SUMMARIZE Use the vocabulary words to write a summary of the lesson.

Test Prep

5. What can be caused by heavy rains?
   A a drought
   B a flood
   C the Grand Canyon
   D mountains

Make Connections

 **Math**

Least to Greatest
Look at the chart. Use the data to order the changes from least amount of time to greatest. Compare the amounts of time it takes for the changes to happen.

Water Changes Land Over Time

Kind of Change	Time It May Take to Happen
flood	a few hours or days
drought	a few months
erosion	many years

237

Holding Dirt in Place

Take a closer look next time you drive by a work site. Look for the low, black material that looks like a fence.

That material is called a silt fence. Workers often dig up dirt, soil, and plants when they work on a road. The loose soil might wash away when it rains. Silt fences hold the loose soil in place.

When the work is finished, workers put the soil into places that need it. That way they save the soil and keep streams from clogging.

Think and Write How do trees and plants keep dirt from washing away?

Don't Fence Me In

Silt fences are made of a special material that holds the soil but lets the water run through.

Find out more. Log on to
www.hspscience.com

Vocabulary Review

Tell which picture goes best with each word.

1. mountain p. 216   **4. stream** p. 226

2. plain p. 218   **5. lake** p. 227

3. beach p. 220   **6. flood** p. 234

A    D

B    E

C    F

Check Understanding

7. Copy and complete this chart.

cause   →   effect

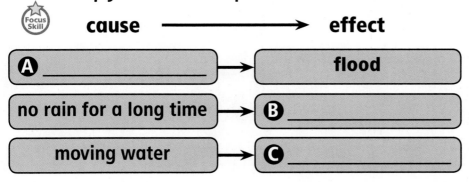

Ⓐ _____ → flood

no rain for a long time → **Ⓑ** _____

moving water → **Ⓒ** _____

8. Where is most of Earth's water?

    A in floods   **B** in lakes

    C in oceans   **D** in rivers

Critical Thinking

9. Put these kinds of land in order from highest to lowest. Tell how you know.

The Big Idea

A

B

C

10. Some people work to stop erosion. Why do you think they do this?

Natural Resources

What's the Big Idea? People use natural resources, such as rocks and water, in different ways.

Essential Questions

Lesson 1

What Are Natural Resources?

Lesson 2

What Can We Observe About Rocks and Soil?

Lesson 3

How Can We Protect Natural Resources?

Go online

Student eBook
www.hspscience.com

What do **YOU** wonder?

Where does water come from? How do you think this helps explain the **Big Idea** for this chapter?

a mountain stream

Investigate to find out about the natural resources in your environment.

Read and Learn about natural resources.

What Are Natural Resources?

Fast Fact

Sailing Ships

Long ago, people used moving air, or wind, to travel in sailing ships. You can observe ways people use natural resources.

natural resource p. 248

sailing ship using wind to move

All Around You

Ask a Question

What are some things in this picture that come from nature?
Investigate to find out. Then read and learn to find out more.

Get Ready

Inquiry Skill Tip

When you observe, you use your senses to find out about things. You can use words and pictures to record what you see.

You need

crayons

construction paper

What to Do

Step 1

Make a chart like this one.

Things I Saw Outdoors	
animals	plants
water	land

Step 2

Go outside. **Observe** everything around you. Draw and label the things that belong in the chart.

Step 3

Share your chart with a classmate. Did you both **observe** the same things?

Draw Conclusions

How is your chart different from your classmate's chart? How is it alike?

Independent Inquiry

Blow into a balloon a few times. **Observe** how much air you breathe out each time.

247

VOCABULARY
natural
    resource

MAIN IDEA AND DETAILS
Look for the main ideas about natural resources.

Natural Resources

A **natural resource** is anything from nature that people can use. Water and air are natural resources. Rocks and soil are natural resources. Plants and animals are natural resources that live on land, in water, and in air.

MAIN IDEA AND DETAILS
What is a natural resource?

What natural resources do you see in this picture?

How are these people using water?

Water

Water is a natural resource that all living things need. People drink water and use it to clean and to cook. People travel on water, too.

 MAIN IDEA AND DETAILS
What are some ways people use water?

Insta-Lab

Can Water Cool You?
Wrap one thermometer in a damp towel. Wrap another in a dry towel. Check them after 10 minutes. Which is cooler? How can you use water to keep your body cool?

249

Air

Air is a natural resource. You can not see air, but it is all around you. Many living things need air to live. People and many animals breathe air. People use air to fill things such as balloons. They also use air to make things move.

 **MAIN IDEA AND DETAILS** What are some ways people use air?

How are these people using air?

What are natural resources?

In this lesson, you learned that air and water are natural resources. You also learned some ways people use them.

1. 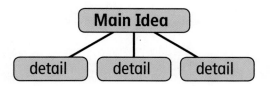 **MAIN IDEA AND DETAILS**
Make a chart like this one. Show details for this main idea. **A natural resource is anything from nature that people can use.**

Main Idea

detail   detail   detail

2. VOCABULARY Use the words **natural resources** to talk about this picture.

3. DRAW CONCLUSIONS Is everything that people use a natural resource? Explain.

4. SUMMARIZE Use the chart to help you write a summary of the lesson. Name some ways people use air and water.

Test Prep
5. How do people use air?
  A They drink it.
  B They build with it.
  C They clean with it.
  D They breathe it.

Make Connections

 Writing

Water Poem
Make a list of sounds that water can make. Use your list to write a poem about water. Draw a picture.

Bath Time
I get in the water — splish, splash, splish!
Soon I'm splashing like a fish.

251

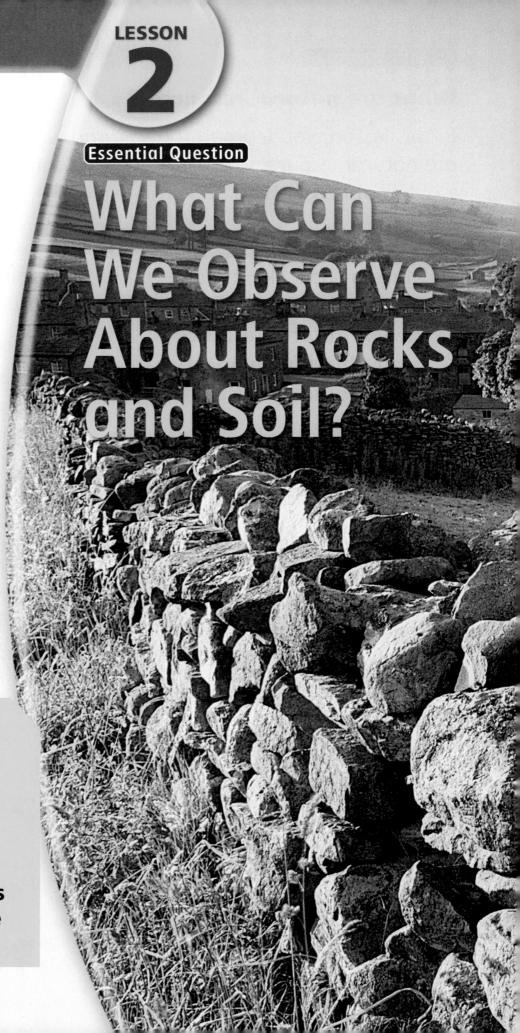

Investigate to find out how rocks can be classified.

Read and Learn about rocks and soil and ways they are used.

Fast Fact

Farm Walls
Farm walls are often made with rocks found in the farm's fields. One way to classify rocks is by where they are found.

What Can We Observe About Rocks and Soil?

rock p. 256

soil p. 258

humus p. 258

farm wall made of rocks

253

Classify Rocks

Ask a Question

How can you classify these rocks?

Investigate to find out. Then read and learn to find out more.

Get Ready

Inquiry Skill Tip

When you classify things, you group them by how they are alike. You can use words to show how you classify things.

You need

hand lens   rocks

What to Do

Step 1

Use a hand lens to observe each rock.

Step 2

Sort the rocks by grouping those that are the same. Make a chart to show how you **classified** the rocks.

Rocks			
White			

Step 3

Use the chart to tell how the rocks are alike. Then tell how they are different.

Draw Conclusions

How are the rocks alike? How are they different?

Independent Inquiry

Using a balance, compare the mass of rocks with ten pennies. **Classify** the rocks by mass.

VOCABULARY
rock
soil
humus

 COMPARE AND CONTRAST
Look for ways rocks and kinds of soil are alike. Also look for ways they are different.

Rocks

A **rock** is a hard, nonliving thing that comes from Earth. Rocks are a natural resource.

The walls of this fort are made of rock.

People use rocks in different ways. They build with rocks. They carve some rocks into statues. Some things from rocks, such as salt, are in the food you eat.

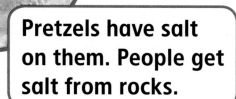

COMPARE AND CONTRAST
Compare some ways people use rocks.

Pretzels have salt on them. People get salt from rocks.

This statue is made of a kind of rock called marble.

Soil

The top layer of Earth is **soil**. Soil is made up of clay, sand, and humus. Clay and sand are small pieces of rock. **Humus** is pieces of dead plants and animals. Soil in different places may have different amounts of sand, humus, and clay.

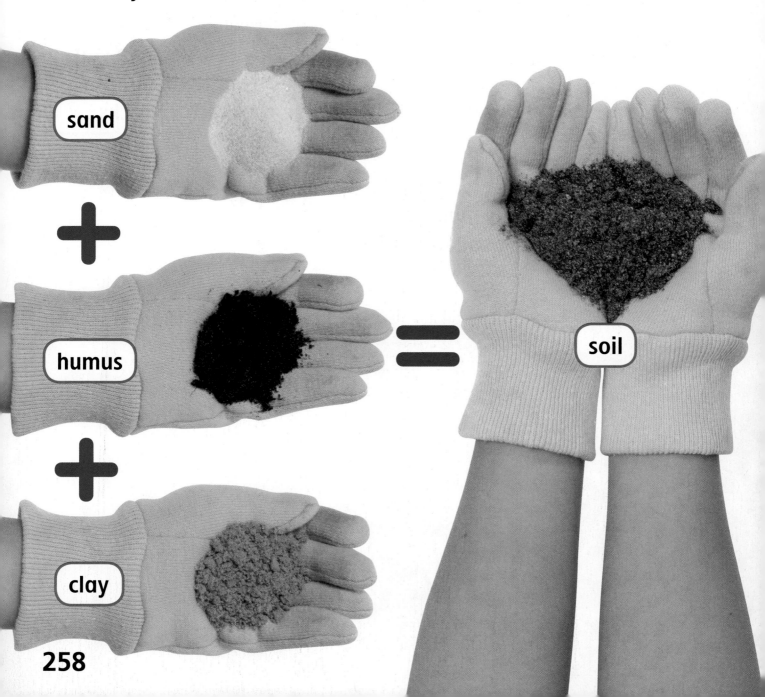

sand

+

humus

+

clay

=

soil

Soil is a natural resource. Some kinds can hold more water than other kinds. People use soil to grow plants. Plants take water and other things they need from soil.

Focus Skill COMPARE AND CONTRAST
How are kinds of soil alike and different?

A girl plants seeds in soil.

Insta-Lab

Hold It!
Put a coffee filter on a cup. Hold it in place with a rubber band. Put soil on the filter. Pour $\frac{1}{2}$ cup of water onto the soil. Measure the water that passes through into the cup. How much water did the soil hold?

Other Things in Soil

Different things may be in soil. Worms and other animals may live there. Plant roots grow down into soil. Pieces of dead plants and animals may be in soil. Small rocks may be in it, too.

Focus Skill **COMPARE AND CONTRAST** Compare some of the different things found in soil.

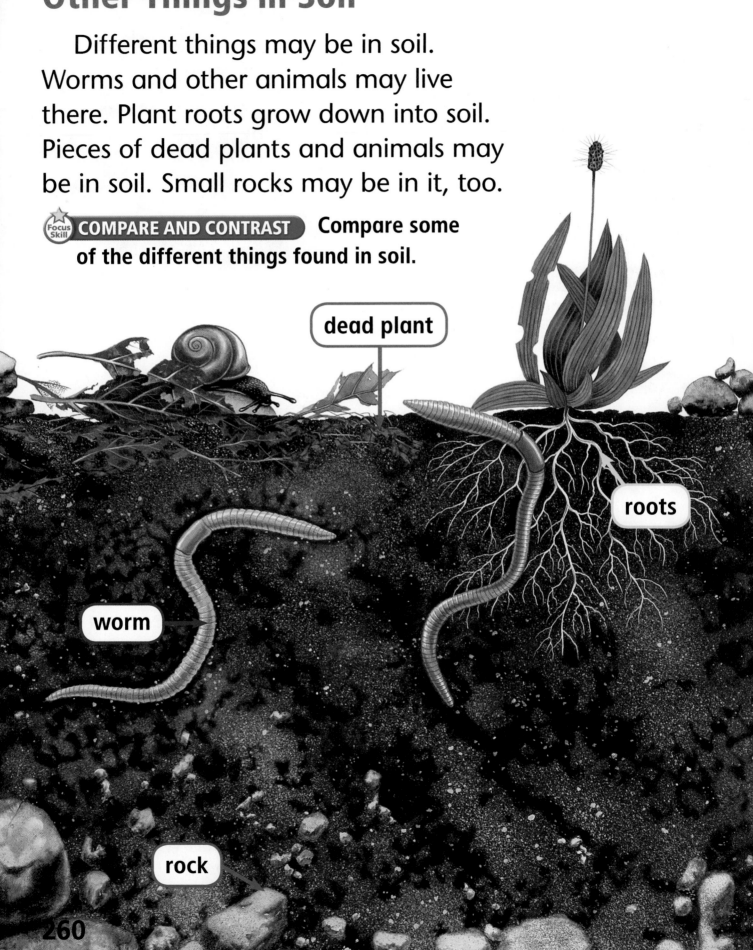

dead plant

roots

worm

rock

Essential Question

What can we observe about rocks and soil?

In this lesson, you learned about ways people use rocks and soil.

1. **Focus Skill** **COMPARE AND CONTRAST** Make a chart like this one. Use it to compare rocks and soil.

alike ——— different

2. VOCABULARY Use the words **rock** and **soil** to tell about this picture.

3. DRAW CONCLUSIONS How can people use soil?

4. SUMMARIZE Use the chart to help you write a summary. Tell about rocks and soil.

Test Prep
5. Why are rocks and soil natural resources?

Make Connections

123 **Math**

Compare Rock and Soil Masses
Get $\frac{1}{2}$ cup of soil and $\frac{1}{2}$ cup of small rocks. Use a balance to compare their masses. Then draw pictures and write >, <, or = to show what you found out.

Investigate to find out how trash harms the land.

Read and Learn about ways to protect Earth's natural resources.

Essential Question

How Can We Protect Natural Resources?

Fast Fact

Recycled Plastic

Some of the things on playgrounds are made from recycled plastic jugs! You can draw a conclusion about why people should recycle things.

pollution p. 266

reduce p. 268

reuse p. 269

recycle p. 269

What things on this playground might be made from recycled plastic?

263

What Happens to Trash?

Ask a Question

Why is it important to put trash in a trash can? Investigate to find out. Then read and learn to find out more.

Get Ready

Inquiry Skill Tip
To draw a conclusion, use what you observe and what you already know to decide what something means.

You need

lettuce

napkin

piece of foam cup

pan of soil

What to Do

Step ①

Bury the lettuce, the napkin, and the piece of foam cup in the soil.

Step ②

Water the soil every three days.

Step ③

After two weeks, dig up the things. What do you observe?

Draw Conclusions

Draw a conclusion. How could trash harm the land? Why?

Independent Inquiry

Make a pencil holder. Draw a conclusion about how your holder helps protect natural resources.

Taking Care of Resources

Pollution harms our natural resources. **Pollution** is waste that causes harm to land, water, and air. Pollution also causes harm to plants and animals.

People can pick up trash on land.

266

People can help take care of natural resources. They can put their trash in trash cans. They can pick up trash they see. They can also walk or ride bikes instead of using cars. Cars and trucks make air pollution and use up natural resources.

 **CAUSE AND EFFECT**
What does pollution cause?

People can walk instead of using cars.

People can pick up trash in water.

Reduce, Reuse, Recycle

People can help care for natural resources. They can reduce, reuse, and recycle. This makes less trash. It also helps save natural resources.

To **reduce** your use of something is to use less of it. People can use cloth bags to reduce the number of paper and plastic bags they use.

To **reuse** is to use something again. People can reuse food jars to hold pencils and other things.

To **recycle** is to use old things to make new things. People can recycle newspapers. The old papers can be made into new paper.

Focus Skill CAUSE AND EFFECT What effect does recycling have on the amount of trash?

Reuse an Egg Carton
Decorate an egg carton. Use it to store things you collect. You can keep different kinds of things in the different cups.

Ways to Save Resources

This family is saving resources. How is each family member helping?

Turn off the lights when you leave a room.

Turn off the water when you do not need it.

Turn down the heat. Put on a sweater to stay warm.

Recycle.

For more links and animations, go to **www.hspscience.com**

How can we protect natural resources?

In this lesson, you learned how pollution harms our natural resources. You also learned ways people can help protect resources.

1. **Focus Skill** **CAUSE AND EFFECT**

Make a chart like this one. Show the effects pollution has on natural resources.

2. VOCABULARY Use the word **pollution** to talk about this picture.

3. DRAW CONCLUSIONS How can you take care of resources at your home?

4. SUMMARIZE Use the vocabulary words to help you write a summary.

Test Prep

5. How do reducing, reusing, and recycling help?

   A They make pollution.

   B They harm land, water, and air.

   C They help save natural resources.

   D They harm plants and animals.

Make Connections

 Math

Counting by Fours

Every person makes about 4 pounds of trash each day. How much would you make in 2 days, in 5 days, and in 1 week? Use a number line or counters to help you count by fours. Show your work in a chart.

How Much Trash?	
days	pounds of trash
1	4
2	8
5	
7	

271

Dr. Ruth Patrick

► **DR. RUTH PATRICK**
► Nature Scientist

Dr. Ruth Patrick is a nature scientist. Her father taught her to love plants, streams, and rivers.

Dr. Patrick looks at how pollution can hurt a river. She studies the plants and animals that live in rivers. She makes a list of things scientists can check to see if a river is polluted. Dr. Patrick helps keep our rivers clean.

 Think and Write

How does Dr. Patrick help keep our rivers clean?

Sylvia Earle

▶ **SYLVIA EARLE**

▶ Studies ocean plants and animals
▶ Marine Biologist

How do you find out what lives in the ocean? You dive in. You observe. You take pictures.

This is just what Sylvia Earle and her teams of scientists do. They dive deep into the Pacific Ocean. They study the plants and animals that live there.

Sylvia Earle wants to protect the living things in the ocean. She studies ways oil spills can harm ocean animals. She helps oil companies keep the ocean clean and safe.

 Think and Write

Why is Sylvia Earle's work important?

Vocabulary Review

Tell which picture goes best with each word or words.

1. natural resource p. 248

A

2. rock p. 256

B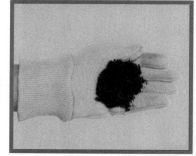

3. humus p. 258

C

4. recycle p. 269

D

Check Understanding

5. Tell the **details** about the natural resources in this picture.

6. Which part of soil is pieces of dead plants and animals?

    A clay   **B** humus

    C rock   **D** soil

7. Which of these harms natural resources?

    F air   **G** humus

    H pollution   **J** recycling

Critical Thinking

8. You want to take care of resources in your school. Write a plan. Tell each thing you would do. Tell how each thing would help.

The Big Idea

Visual Summary

Tell how each picture shows the **Big Idea** for its chapter.

CHAPTER 5 Big Idea

Earth has landforms and bodies of water. Water can change Earth.

CHAPTER 6 Big Idea

People use natural resources, such as rocks and water, in different ways.

Weather, Seasons, and the Sky

Unit Inquiry

Starry, Starry Night

As you read this unit, you will find out about objects in the sky. Plan and do a test. Find out how the nighttime sky is different from the daytime sky.

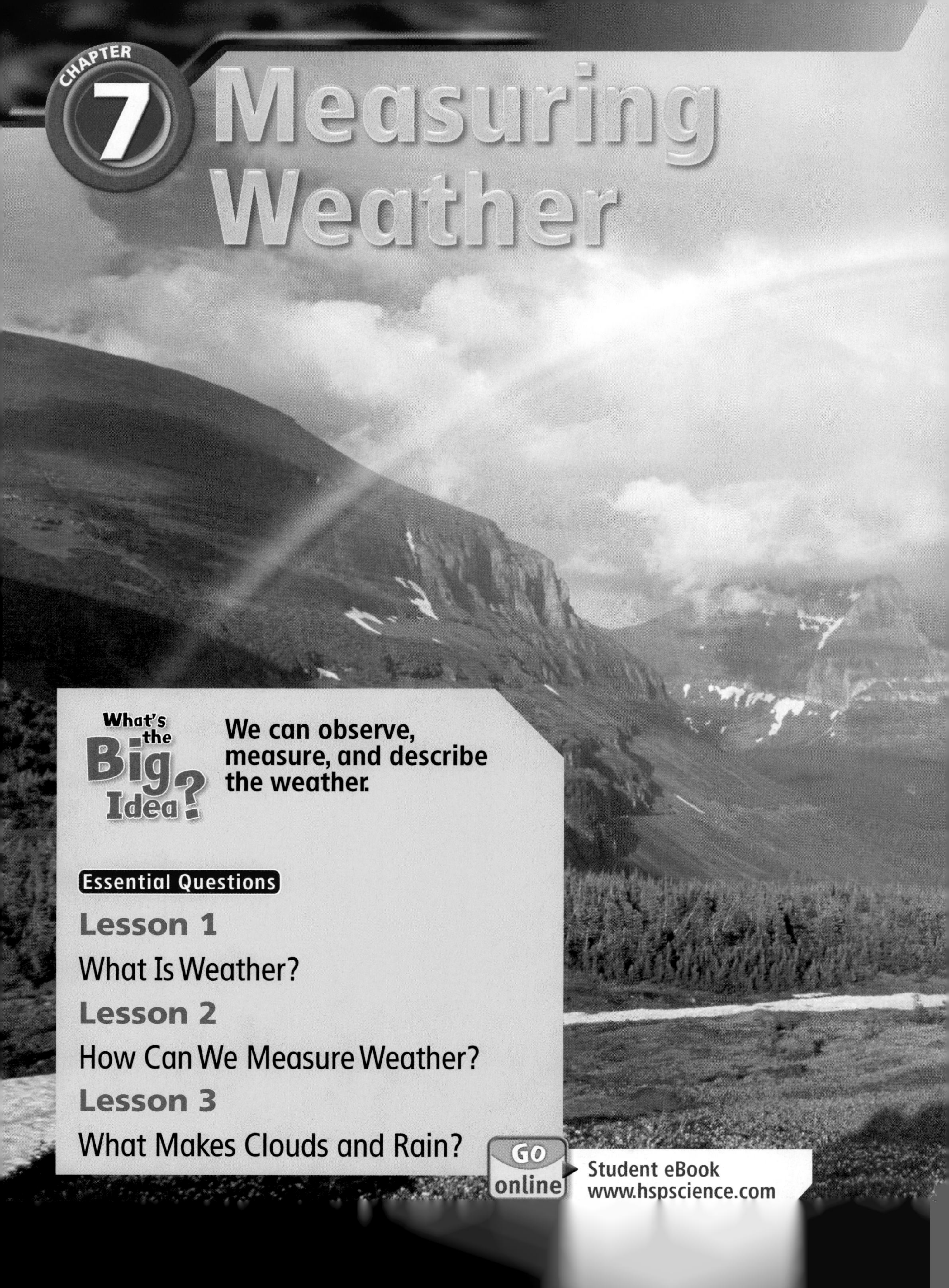

What's the Big Idea?

We can observe, measure, and describe the weather.

Essential Questions

GO online Student eBook
www.hspscience.com

Investigate to find out why weather changes from day to day.

Read and Learn about kinds of weather and how it can change from day to day.

Essential Question

What Is Weather?

Fast Fact

Snow

About 25 centimeters (10 inches) of snow equals about 3 centimeters (1 inch) of rain. You can compare the kinds of weather from day to day.

weather p. 284

cold, snowy day

Daily Weather

Ask a Question

What is the weather in the photograph like?
Investigate to find out.
Then read and learn to find out more.

Get Ready

Inquiry Skill Tip

When you compare, you look for ways things are alike and different. You can draw pictures or use words to show how you compared things.

You need

paper

markers

What to Do

Step ①

Observe the weather each day for two weeks.

Step ②

Make a chart. Record what you see.

Step ③

Compare the weather from day to day. Do you see any patterns? Predict next week's weather.

Draw Conclusions

How is the weather alike from day to day? How is it different?

Independent Inquiry

Blow on the back of your hand. Spray some water on your other hand and then blow. Compare how they feel.

VOCABULARY
weather

 COMPARE AND CONTRAST

Look for ways in which the weather can be different from day to day.

Weather

Weather is what the air outside is like. You can see and feel the weather. It may be warm or cool. It may be snowy, windy, rainy, cloudy, or sunny.

What kinds of weather do you see on this page?

Weather can change. It may be sunny one day. The next day it may be cloudy. It may be cold for many days. Then it may warm up. One day may be windy. Another day may be calm.

Focus Skill · COMPARE AND CONTRAST

How can weather be different from day to day?

Insta-Lab

Observing Weather

Look out the window. Observe the sky. Observe what people are wearing. What can you tell about the weather? Do this each day for a week. Make a chart to show your weather data.

Weather and You

In cold weather, you wear clothes that keep you warm. In warm weather, you wear clothes that keep you cool. When it rains, you wear clothes that keep you dry. You choose activities to go with the weather, too.

Focus Skill COMPARE AND CONTRAST

How is clothing for cold weather different from clothing for warm weather?

What activities are these people doing?

What is weather?

In this lesson, you learned that weather may be sunny, rainy, cloudy, windy, or snowy. You also learned that it can change from day to day.

1. **COMPARE AND CONTRAST**

Make a chart like this one. Use it to compare kinds of weather.

alike ——— different

2. VOCABULARY

Use the word **weather** to tell about this picture.

3. **DRAW CONCLUSIONS** How should you dress for each kind of weather?

4. **SUMMARIZE** Use the chart to help you write a summary. Tell about weather.

Test Prep

5. In what weather do you wear clothes that keep you cool?

A cold   **B** rainy

C snowy   **D** warm

Make Connections

 Writing

Weather Poem

Think about your favorite kind of weather. Write a poem. Start each line with a letter of a word that goes with that weather. Tell why you like that kind of weather.

Snow is all around.
No school.
Outside we make a snowman
We play all day.

How Can We Measure Weather?

Investigate to find out the temperatures of different places.

Read and Learn about how you can use special tools to measure the weather.

Fast Fact

Weather Vane
This tool shows the direction of the wind. How else do people measure weather?

temperature
p. 292

thermometer
p. 292

weather vane

Measure Temperature

Guided Inquiry

Ask a Question

What are the people in this picture measuring? What tool are they using?
Investigate to find out. Then read and learn to find out more.

Get Ready

Inquiry Skill Tip

When you measure, you find the size or amount of something. You can use numbers to record what you find.

You need

thermometer

red crayon

What to Do

Step ①

Draw two thermometers. Label one **inside** and one **outside**.

Step ②

Measure the temperature inside and outside the classroom. Record on the thermometers you drew.

Step ③

How do your **measurements** help you know where it is warmer?

Draw Conclusions

Where is the temperature warmer?

Independent Inquiry

Make your own rain gauge. **Measure** the amount of rain that falls once a week for four weeks.

Focus Skill MAIN IDEA AND DETAILS
Look for the main ideas about measuring weather.

Measuring Temperature

One way to measure weather is to find the temperature. **Temperature** is the measure of how hot or cold something is. A **thermometer** is a tool for measuring temperature.

Focus Skill MAIN IDEA AND DETAILS How can you find out how warm the air is outside?

thermometer

Measuring Rain

You can also measure how much rain falls. This tool is a rain gauge. It shows how much rain has fallen.

 **MAIN IDEA AND DETAILS**

How can you measure rain?

rain gauge

Insta-Lab

Where's the Heat?

Find the warmest place in your classroom. Use a thermometer. Measure the temperature in different places. Tell what you find out.

Measuring Wind

You can measure wind, too. An anemometer measures the speed of the wind. A weather vane shows the direction of the wind. A windsock also shows the direction of the wind.

Focus Skill MAIN IDEA AND DETAILS

What are two tools that measure the direction of wind?

weather vane

anemometer

windsocks

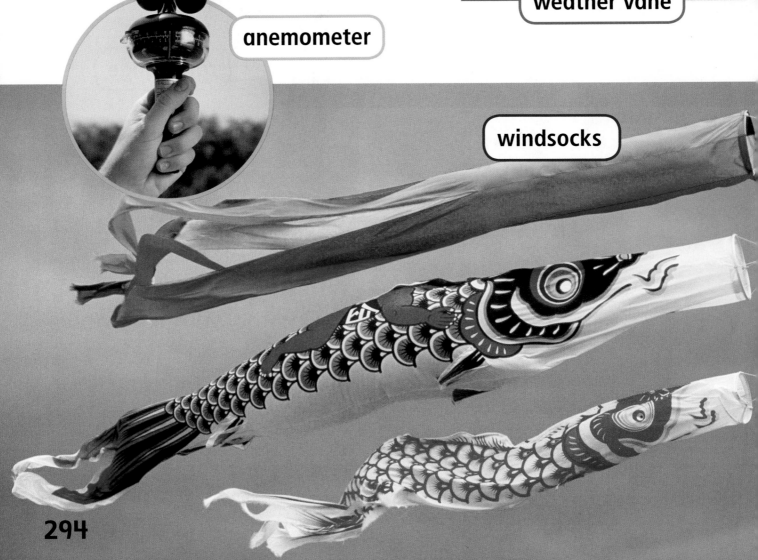

Essential Question

How can we measure weather?

In this lesson, you learned that we can use a thermometer, a rain gauge, an anemometer and a weather vane to measure the weather.

1. **MAIN IDEA AND DETAILS** Make a chart like this one. Show details for this main idea. **You can measure weather in many ways.**

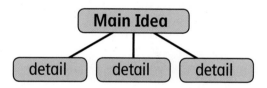

2. VOCABULARY Use the words **temperature** and **thermometer** to tell about the picture.

3. DRAW CONCLUSIONS How can measuring weather help people?

4. SUMMARIZE Use the chart to help you write a summary. Name some tools you can use to measure weather.

Test Prep

5. What are three ways you can measure weather?

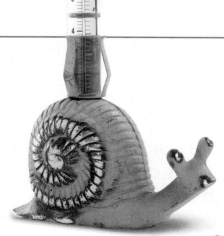

Make Connections

123 Math

Solve Problems

Juan's rain gauge showed 5 centimeters Monday and 3 more Tuesday. How much rain fell in all?

Investigate to find out how clouds form.

Read and Learn about clouds and the water cycle.

Essential Question

What Makes Clouds and Rain?

Fast Fact

Rain Clouds

Rain clouds look dark because they are thick and block the sun. What can you infer about clouds and rain?

water cycle
p. 300

evaporate p. 300

water vapor
p. 300

condense p. 300

dark rain clouds

Make Clouds

Ask a Question

How do you think these clouds formed? Investigate to find out. Then read and learn to find out more.

Get Ready

Inquiry Skill Tip

When you infer, you use what you observed to tell why something happened.

You need

jar with lid

hot water

ice cubes

What to Do

Step ➊

Let your teacher put the hot water in the jar. Wait one minute. Then pour most of it out. CAUTION: hot water!

Step ➋

Turn the jar lid upside down. Place it on the jar. Observe.

Step ➌

Place ice on the lid. Observe. **Infer** how clouds form.

Draw Conclusions

What caused the cloud to form?

Independent Inquiry

Place a jar with ice water in a warm spot. Observe. **Infer** where the water on the outside came from.

VOCABULARY
water cycle   water vapor
evaporate   condense

Focus Skill CAUSE AND EFFECT
Look for what causes clouds
and rain to form.

The Water Cycle

Clouds and rain are part of the water cycle. In the **water cycle**, water moves from Earth to the air and back again.

Focus Skill CAUSE AND EFFECT
What causes water to evaporate?

Science Up Close

The Water Cycle

1 The sun makes water warm. This causes the water to **evaporate**, or change to water vapor. **Water vapor** is water in the air that you can not see.

2 Water vapor meets cool air. The cool air causes the water vapor to **condense**, or change into tiny water drops. The drops form clouds.

300

3 Water drops come together and get bigger and heavier. Then they fall as rain or snow.

4 Some rain and snow falls into rivers, lakes, and oceans. Some flows there from the land.

5 The cycle continues.

For more links and animations, go to **www.hspscience.com**

Clouds

Clouds are clues about how the weather may change.

CAUSE AND EFFECT
What kind of clouds bring rain or snow?

Clouds	Weather
 cumulus	Some clouds look like puffy white cotton. They often mean nice weather.
 stratus	Other clouds are gray, flat, and low in the sky. They may bring rain or snow.
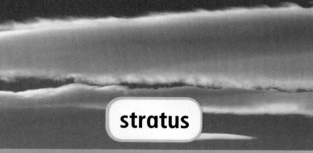 cirrus	These clouds look like thin, white feathers. They often mean sunny weather.

What makes clouds and rain?

In this lesson, you learned how the water cycle works. You also learned that cumulus, stratus, and cirrus clouds can help predict the weather.

1. 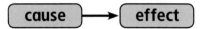 **CAUSE AND EFFECT**
Make a chart like this one. Show the causes and effects of the water cycle.

2. VOCABULARY Use the word **condense** to tell about this picture.

3. DRAW CONCLUSIONS
What will the weather be like if you see cirrus clouds in the sky?

4. SUMMARIZE Use the vocabulary words to help you write a summary.

Test Prep
5. In what does water move from the land to the air and back again?
A in the water cycle
B in the ocean
C in the clouds
D in the rain

Make Connections

 **Math**

Use Ordinal Numbers
Work with a partner to draw the steps of the water cycle. Write about each step. First, the sun heats the water. Use **second**, **third**, and **fourth** to retell the other steps.

303

June Bacon-Bercey

▶ **JUNE BACON-BERCEY**

▶ Meteorologist
▶ Expert on weather and flying

June Bacon-Bercey is a science teacher in California. Many of her students do not know that she is also a famous weather scientist.

June Bacon-Bercey started as a TV weather reporter. Later, she became an expert on weather and how it affects flying. She has won awards. She also has started an award of her own. Each year, this award gives money to a woman who wants to become a weather scientist like herself.

 Think and Write

Why is weather important to flying?

Meteorologists

Meteorologists are weather scientists. They can tell when the weather will change. They study weather patterns to predict when a thunderstorm might happen. Thunderstorms can bring strong wind and heavy rain. They can harm people and their homes. If people know when bad weather is coming, they can make plans to stay safe. Meteorologists help people do that.

✎ Think and Write

Why is predicting the weather important?

Vocabulary Review

Use these words to complete the sentences.

weather p. 284   **evaporate** p. 300

thermometer p. 292   **water vapor** p. 300

1. A tool that measures temperature is a _____.

2. Warmth may cause water to _____.

3. Water in the air is _____.

4. The way the air is outside is _____.

Check Understanding

5. What is the **cause** for each **effect** labeled with an arrow in the water cycle?

6. Which tool would you use to find out how fast the wind is blowing?

A anemometer

C thermometer

B rain gauge

D weather vane

7. What do clouds give clues about?

    F the temperature

    G how windy it is

    H how much it will rain

    J what the weather will be

Critical Thinking

8. You are getting dressed for school. How can you make sure you wear the right clothes for the weather?

The **Big Idea**

Seasons

The four seasons all have their own kind of weather.

Essential Questions

Student eBook
www.hspscience.com

Why do some leaves change color? How do you think this connects to the **Big Idea** for this chapter?

a fall day

Investigate to find out what plants need to help them grow.

Read and Learn about the weather in spring and how it affects plants and animals.

(Essential Question)

What Is Spring?

Fast Fact

Spring Garden
Early spring is the best time to plant a vegetable garden. You can hypothesize about what helps plants grow in spring.

season p. 314

spring p. 316

garden in springtime

Plants and Light

Ask a Question

Why did this plant grow the way it did?
Investigate to find out. Then read and learn to find out more.

Get Ready

Inquiry Skill Tip

When you hypothesize, you tell why you think something will happen. Then you test your idea.

You need

young plant

shoe box with hole

spray bottle

What to Do

Step ①

Put the plant in the box. Put the lid on the box.

Step ②

Place the box so that the hole faces a window. **Hypothesize** about what will happen to the plant.

Step ③

Spray the plant with water each day. After one week, what happens? Was your **hypothesis** correct?

Draw Conclusions

After another week, what happens? Explain.

Independent Inquiry

Which helps seeds sprout in spring—sun or water? **Hypothesize.** Investigate and then explain your results.

VOCABULARY
season
spring

Focus Skill **MAIN IDEA AND DETAILS**
Look for the main ideas about spring.

Seasons

A **season** is a time of year. A year has four seasons. The seasons are spring, summer, fall, and winter. They form a pattern. After every winter comes spring.

Science Up Close

Seasons

Spring starts in the month of March.

314

spring

summer

fall

winter

For more links and animations,
go to **www.hspscience.com**

Spring

Spring is the season after winter. In spring, the weather gets warmer. There may be many rainy days. Spring has more hours of daylight than winter. People may go outside more.

Focus Skill MAIN IDEA AND DETAILS

What is the weather like in spring?

rain

How can you tell it is spring?

Plants in Spring

Many plants begin to grow in spring. They get more warmth, light, and rain in spring than in winter. Plants may grow new leaves and flowers.

Focus Skill MAIN IDEA AND DETAILS

Why do many plants grow well in spring?

flowers

flowering tree

Animals in Spring

Spring is a good time for many animals to have their young. New plants are food for the young. Some young animals are born. Others hatch from eggs. It is easy for them all to find food.

geese and goslings

Focus Skill **MAIN IDEA AND DETAILS**

Why is spring a good time for animals to have their young?

ewe and lambs

318

What is spring?

In this lesson, you learned that the four seasons form a pattern. You also learned what happens to plants and animals in spring.

1. 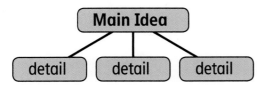 **MAIN IDEA AND DETAILS**
Make a chart like this one. Show details for this main idea. **Spring is one of the four seasons.**

2. VOCABULARY
Tell about the **season** in this picture.

3. DRAW CONCLUSIONS
What season comes after winter every year? How do you know?

4. SUMMARIZE Use the chart to help you write a summary. Tell about spring.

Test Prep
5. What helps plants grow in spring?
   A freezing weather
   B seasons
   C warmth, light, and rain
   D young animals

Make Connections

 Writing

Spring Stories
Write a story about a young animal in spring. Tell what the animal sees and does. Use what you know about animals in spring to write your story.

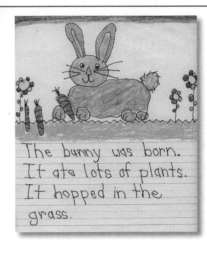

The bunny was born. It ate lots of plants. It hopped in the grass.

What Is Summer?

Investigate to find out the kinds of activities people do in summer.

Read and Learn about the weather in summer and how it affects plants and animals.

Fast Fact

Collecting Shells

There are more kinds of shells than you can count. Many people collect shells in summer. You can infer why people do different activities in different seasons.

summer p. 324

collecting shells in summer

Hot Weather Activities

Ask a Question

How do you know that it is summer in the picture? Investigate to find out. Then read and learn to find out more.

Get Ready

Inquiry Skill Tip

When you infer, you use what you observed to tell why something happened.

You need

seasons
picture cards

What to Do

Step ① ==========

Work with a partner.
Talk about what people
do in summer.

Step ② ==========

Look at each card. Find
clues that tell about
the season. **Infer** which
pictures show summer.

Step ③

Compare your ideas with
other classmates' ideas.
How do you know which
pictures show summer?

Draw Conclusions

What clues help you know
that the activities happen
in the summer?

Independent Inquiry

Spray two towels with
water. Put one in a warm
place and the other in a
cool place. **Infer** what
can happen in the hot
sun.

VOCABULARY
summer

 **MAIN IDEA AND DETAILS**
Look for the main ideas about summer.

Summer

Summer is the season after spring. It has even more hours of daylight. Summer weather can be hot. People dress to keep cool. Some places may have thunderstorms.

MAIN IDEA AND DETAILS
What is summer?

hot weather

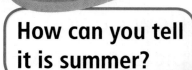

How can you tell it is summer?

Plants in Summer

Summer weather helps many plants grow. Trees have many green leaves. Some plants grow fruits.

 **MAIN IDEA AND DETAILS**
How do plants change in summer?

tomato plant

trees with leaves

Animals in Summer

In summer, animals have ways to stay cool. Some cool off in mud or water. Others lose fur so that their coats are lighter.

Young animals can find all the food they need. They grow bigger.

pig cooling off in mud

 **MAIN IDEA AND DETAILS**

What is one way animals stay cool in summer?

bison shedding fur

Essential Question

What is summer?

In this lesson, you learned what the weather is like in summer. You also learned what happens to plants and animals in summer.

1. 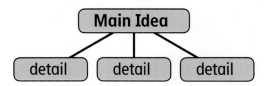 **MAIN IDEA AND DETAILS**
Make a chart like this one. Show details for this main idea. **Summer is the season after spring.**

```
        Main Idea
    ┌───────┼───────┐
 detail   detail   detail
```

2. VOCABULARY
Use the word **summer** to tell about the picture.

3. DRAW CONCLUSIONS
Why do some people like cold drinks in summer?

4. SUMMARIZE Write two sentences to summarize the lesson. Tell about plants and animals in summer.

Test Prep
5. Write about how plants change from spring to summer.

Make Connections

 **Math**

Use a Calendar
Use a calendar to answer these questions. How many months are there? Which ones are summer months? When does summer begin?

JUNE						
SUN	MON	TUE	WED	THU	FRI	SAT
			1	2	3	4
5	6	7	8	9	10	11
12	13	14	15	16	17	18
19	20	21	22	23	24	25
26	27	28	29	30		

Investigate to find out how kinds of seeds are alike and different.

Read and Learn about the weather in fall and how it affects plants and animals.

What Is Fall?

Fast Fact

Apples in the Fall

Apples get ripe in fall. People pick the apples and make them into foods to eat all year. You can compare fruits in many ways.

fall p. 332

migrate p. 334

apple picking in the fall

329

Compare Seeds

Ask a Question

Look at the photograph of the pumpkin seeds. How would you describe them? Investigate to find out. Then read and learn to find out more.

Get Ready

Inquiry Skill Tip
When you compare objects, you see how they are alike and different. You can draw pictures to show how you compared the objects.

You need

fruits with seeds

hand lens

What to Do

Step ① Look at the fruits with the hand lens. Find the seeds. **Compare** the seeds. How are they alike? How are they different?

Step ② Draw and label pictures of the fruits and seeds.

Step ③ Talk about how the seeds are alike. Then talk about how they are different.

Draw Conclusions

Do all seeds look the same? Explain.

Independent Inquiry

Put some apple rings on a string. Put others in a sealed bag. After a week, **compare** the rings.

VOCABULARY
fall
migrate

 CAUSE AND EFFECT
Look for reasons that plants and animals change in fall.

Fall

Fall is the season after summer. It has fewer hours of daylight than summer. The temperature gets cooler. People dress to keep warm.

 CAUSE AND EFFECT
Why do people wear more clothes in fall?

How can you tell it is fall?

cleaning up leaves

332

Plants in Fall

In many places, leaves change color and fall from the trees. This happens because they do not get as much daylight as in summer.

Some fruits get ripe in fall. Then they are ready to pick and eat.

Focus Skill **CAUSE AND EFFECT**
Why do we pick some fruits in fall?

Swim!
Why do you swim in summer more than in fall? Put a cup of water under a lamp. **CAUTION:** The lamp may be hot! Put another cup of water in a shady place. Which cup of water warms up faster?

squashes

maple trees

333

Animals in Fall

As the air gets cooler, food may be harder for animals to find. Some animals store food to eat later. Others **migrate**, or move to new places, to find food.

 **CAUSE AND EFFECT**

Why do some animals store food in fall?

squirrel carrying food

geese migrating

Essential Question

What is fall?

In this lesson, you learned what the weather is like in fall. You also learned what happens to plants and animals in fall.

1. **Focus Skill** **CAUSE AND EFFECT**
Make a chart like this one. Show how changes in fall affect people and animals.

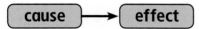

2. **VOCABULARY** Use the word **fall** to tell about these fruits.

3. **DRAW CONCLUSIONS** Why do the leaves in some places change color and drop off the trees in fall?

4. **SUMMARIZE** Use the chart to help you write a summary. Tell what happens in fall.

Test Prep
5. Why do some animals move to new places in fall?
  A to stay cool
  B to find food
  C to grow seeds
  D to have their young

Make Connections

 Writing

Apple Book
Work with a partner to draw healthful snacks that are made with apples. Write a sentence for each picture. Bind the pictures together to make a book.

335

Investigate to find out how you can stay warm in winter.

Read and Learn about the weather in winter and how it affects plants and animals.

Essential Question

What Is Winter?

Fast Fact

Trees in Winter
Some trees stay green all year, even in winter. Draw a conclusion about what happens to plants and animals in winter.

winter p. 340

snow-covered trees in winter

How to Stay Warm

Guided Inquiry

Ask a Question

Why are the people in the picture dressed the way they are?
Investigate to find out. Then read and learn to find out more.

Get Ready

Inquiry Skill Tip

To draw a conclusion, use what you observe and what you already know to decide what something means.

You need

plastic bag

ice water

mitten

What to Do

Step ①

Put your hand in the bag. Dip the bag into the water. How does your hand feel?

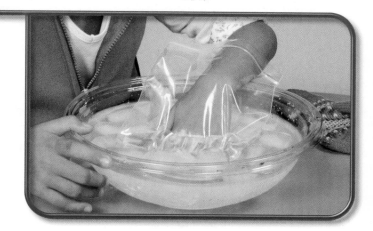

Step ②

Put on the mitten. Put your hand in the bag.

Step ③

Dip the bag into the water. How does your hand feel?

Draw Conclusions

Draw a conclusion about what can keep you warm in winter.

Independent Inquiry

Talk about foods you eat in winter. Draw a conclusion about why these foods are good to eat in winter.

VOCABULARY
winter

Focus Skill MAIN IDEA AND DETAILS
Look for the main ideas
about winter.

Winter

Winter is the season after fall. Winter has the fewest hours of daylight. In some places, the air is cold. Snow may fall. People in these places wear many extra clothes. In other places, the air may just get cooler.

Focus Skill MAIN IDEA AND DETAILS
How is winter different
from fall?

How can you tell
it is winter?

Plants in Winter

Many plants have no leaves in winter. Other plants stay green.

Some plants rest. They do not grow until it gets warm again. Other plants die.

 MAIN IDEA AND DETAILS

What can happen to plants in the winter?

Cold-Weather Clothes

Draw a picture of yourself in very cold weather. Label each thing you wear to stay warm. Then show your work to a partner. Tell how each piece of clothing keeps you warm.

holly

bare tree

Animals in Winter

Food can be hard to find in winter. Some animals eat food that they stored in fall. Others sleep until spring.

Some animals change color to stay safe. Some grow thick coats to stay warm.

Focus Skill **MAIN IDEA AND DETAILS**
How do some animals change in winter?

This animal changes color in winter.

This animal grows a thick coat in winter.

What is winter?

In this lesson, you learned what the weather is like in winter. You also learned what happens to plants and animals in winter.

1. 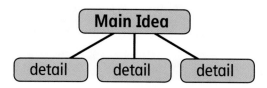 **MAIN IDEA AND DETAILS** Make a chart like this one. Show details for this main idea. **Winter is the season after fall.**

```
        Main Idea
      /     |     \
 detail  detail  detail
```

2. VOCABULARY Tell how you know this picture shows **winter**.

3. DRAW CONCLUSIONS Why do you think it is hard for animals to find food in winter?

4. SUMMARIZE Use the chart to help you write a summary. Tell what happens to plants and animals in winter.

Test Prep
5. How can winter be different in different places?

Make Connections

 Social Studies

Snowy Places
Look at a map of the United States. Find places where it snows in winter. Make a list of these places. Tell how they are alike.

It snows in
1. New York
2. Maine
3. Montana

Snow Is Useful

When snow falls, it is soft and fluffy. Over time, it gets packed down hard.

Snow is strong and does not let cold through it. People in the far North use it to build shelters called igloos when they travel.

The Inuit

Canada is a country north of the United States. In the far North of Canada, there is a group of people called Inuit. Sometimes the Inuit have to travel during the winter. They move across large areas of snow and ice. When they stop for the night, they need a shelter.

A tent would not keep out the cold. So the Inuit use snow to build an igloo.

The Inuit cut snow into blocks. Then they stack the blocks into a curved shape. They use more snow to fill the cracks. Outside the door, they build a low tunnel. They crawl through this to go in. The tunnel stops the wind from blowing in.

✍ Think and Write

Why do you think igloos are built only during the winter?

- The largest snowflake ever seen was more than a foot across.

- No two snowflakes are alike.

- All snowflakes have six sides.

- Stampede Pass, Washington, is the snow capital of the United States!

Spin-In™

Find out more. Log on to
www.hspscience.com

Review and Test Prep

Vocabulary Review

Match the word to its picture.

1. spring p. 316   **3.** fall p. 332

2. summer p. 324 **4.** winter p. 340

Check Understanding

5. What is a season? Tell **details** about one season.

6. In which season would you see trees with many green leaves? Tell why.

7. Why do some animals shed some of their fur in summer?

    A to stay warm

    B to hide

    C to find food

    D to stay cool

Critical Thinking

8. Tell how the tree changes with each season.

Objects in the Sky

What's the Big Idea?

The sun, moon, and stars are objects in the sky that seem to move because Earth rotates.

Essential Questions

Lesson 1

What Can We See in the Sky?

Lesson 2

What Causes Day and Night?

Lesson 3

What Can We Observe About the Moon?

GO online ▸ **Student eBook**
www.hspscience.com

moon in the daytime sky

What do **you** wonder?

Why can you sometimes see the moon in the daytime? How do you think this connects to the **Big Idea** for this chapter?

349

Investigate to find out what objects can be seen in the daytime sky.

Read and Learn about objects that can be seen in the daytime and nighttime skies.

What Can We See in the Sky?

Fast Fact

Stars

Moving air causes some of the light from the stars to bend. This makes the stars seem to twinkle. You can communicate about what you see in the sky.

twinkling stars

Vocabulary Preview

sun p. 354

star p. 354

moon p. 355

351

The Daytime Sky

Ask a Question

Which objects can be seen in the daytime sky? Which object can sometimes be seen in the nighttime sky?
Investigate to find out. Then read and learn to find out more.

Get Ready

Inquiry Skill Tip

You can use pictures, numbers, or writing to communicate what you observe.

You need

colored paper

crayons

What to Do

Step 1

Look out the window.
Observe the daytime sky.

Step 2

Draw pictures of what
you see. Write about it.

Step 3

Share your work with a
partner. Use it to help you
communicate what you
observed.

Draw Conclusions

What objects did you see?
What objects did your
partner see?

Independent Inquiry

Observe the sky at
sunset. Draw and
write what you see.
Communicate what you
observed.

353

VOCABULARY
sun
star
moon

 COMPARE AND CONTRAST
Look for ways the daytime and nighttime skies are alike and ways they are different.

Observing the Sky

In the daytime sky, you may see clouds and the sun. The **sun** is the star closest to Earth. A **star** is an object in the sky that gives off its own light. The sun lights Earth.

sun

clouds

In the nighttime sky, you may see stars, planets, and the moon. The **moon** is a huge ball of rock. It does not give off its own light. Its light comes from the sun.

moon

(Focus Skill) **COMPARE AND CONTRAST**

How are the daytime sky and the nighttime sky different?

planet

stars

Insta-Lab

Moonlight

Cover a ball with foil. Have a partner shine a flashlight at the ball. Does the ball seem brighter when it is lit up? How is the ball like the moon? How is the flashlight like the sun?

Telescopes

You can look at the sky with a telescope. A telescope is a tool that makes things that are far away look closer. It can help you see more of the moon, stars, and planets.

Look at the planet Mars with just your eyes. This is what you see.

Look at Mars with a telescope. This is what you see. How much more can you see now?

For more links and animations, go to **www.hspscience.com**

What can we see in the sky?

In this lesson, you learned about the sun, the moon, and the stars. You also learned that you can use a telescope to see objects in the nighttime sky.

1. (Focus Skill) **COMPARE AND CONTRAST** Make a chart like this one. Use it to compare objects seen in the sky.

(alike)————(different)

2. VOCABULARY Use the words **sun** and **star** to talk about this picture.

3. DRAW CONCLUSIONS Why do you think the sun is much brighter than the moon?

4. SUMMARIZE Use the chart to help you write a summary. Tell about objects in the sky.

Test Prep

5. What does a telescope do?

A It makes things that are far away look closer.

B It makes things that are close look farther away.

C It makes very big things look farther away.

D It makes very big things look smaller.

Make Connections

 Writing

Stories About the Sky
Long ago, people made up stories about what they saw in the sky. Write your own sky story, and draw a picture to go with it.

The sun is a happy teacher. The clouds are her students.

Investigate to model day and night on Earth.

Read and Learn about what causes day and night.

Essential Question

What Causes Day and Night?

Fast Fact

Day and Night
When it is daytime in the United States, it is nighttime in China. You can make a model to see why this happens.

rotate p. 362

**daytime on one side of Earth
and nighttime on the other**

Model Day and Night

Ask a Question

How did this city go from day to night?
Investigate to find out. Then read and learn to find out more.

Get Ready

You need

labels

tape

globe

flashlight

What to Do

Step ①

Label the globe **Earth**. Label the flashlight **sun**. Use them to make a model of Earth and the sun.

Step ②

Make the room dark. Have a partner hold the globe. Shine the flashlight on it.

Step ③

How does the model help you see why Earth has day and night?

Draw Conclusions

What would happen if your partner turned the globe?

Independent Inquiry

Make a model to show how Earth rotates. Label your country. Rotate the globe. Observe what happens.

VOCABULARY
rotate

 **CAUSE AND EFFECT**
Look for what causes day and night.

Day and Night

Each day, the sun seems to move across the sky. It is not the sun that is moving. It is Earth! Earth rotates. To **rotate** is to spin like a top.

United States

day

As Earth rotates, the side we live on turns toward the sun. The sun lights the sky, and we have day. As Earth keeps rotating, our side turns away from the sun. The sky gets dark, and we have night.

(Focus Skill) CAUSE AND EFFECT

What do we have when the side of Earth we live on turns toward the sun? Why?

United States

night

Objects in the Sky Seem to Move

The sun, moon, and stars seem to move in the sky. As Earth spins, we turn toward and away from the sun, moon, and stars. We can not feel that we are moving, so it seems to us as if the sun, moon, and stars do move.

 **CAUSE AND EFFECT**

Why does the sun seem to move in the sky?

Things Seem to Move

Stand in an open space. Turn around in circles. Do the things around you seem to move? How is this like the way the sun and stars seem to move around Earth?

noon

morning

evening

364

Essential Question

What causes day and night?

In this lesson, you learned that the sun, the moon, and the stars all seem to move across the sky. We just see them in different places because Earth is rotating. Earth's rotating also causes day and night.

1. **Focus Skill** CAUSE AND EFFECT
Make a chart like this one. Show what causes day and night.

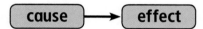

cause ⟶ effect

2. VOCABULARY Use the word **rotate** to talk about this picture.

3. DRAW CONCLUSIONS What do we have when the side of Earth we live on turns away from the sun? Why?

4. SUMMARIZE Use the chart to help you write a summary. Tell about day and night.

Test Prep

5. Why do we have daytime when China has nighttime?

Make Connections

123 Math

Time and the Sun
Observe the sun at 8:00 A.M., noon, and 7:00 P.M. Draw and write about what you observe. Will the sun be in about the same places at the same times tomorrow? Why? Check tomorrow to see if you were right.

Investigate to find out how craters on the moon are made.

Read and Learn about why the moon seems to change shape.

What Can We Observe About the Moon?

Fast Fact

Craters on the Moon

Much of the moon is covered with dust. It has many craters. You can use what you know to infer how the craters were made.

crater p. 372

surface of the moon

367

The Surface of the Moon

Guided Inquiry

Ask a Question

How do you think this crater was formed?

Investigate to find out. Then read and learn to find out more.

Get Ready

Inquiry Skill Tip

When you infer, you use what you observed to tell why something happened.

You need

pan of sand

spray bottle of water

marbles

What to Do

Step ① Spray the sand lightly with water.

Step ② Hold the marbles above the sand. Drop them one at a time. Observe.

Step ③ Infer how the moon's craters were made. Compare your ideas with others' ideas.

Draw Conclusions

What objects in space could make craters on the moon?

Independent Inquiry

Compare the moon's surface with Earth's surface. Infer why people do not live on the moon.

VOCABULARY
crater

 **SEQUENCE**

Look for the pattern in which the moon seems to change.

Changes in the Moon's Shape

The shape of the moon seems to change a little each night. The changes make a pattern that takes about 29 days.

On some nights, you can not see the moon at all. Then you start to see a little of it. After about 15 days, you see the moon as a full circle. Then you see less of it each night. In about 14 more days, you can not see it again.

Day 22
quarter moon

SEQUENCE What happens to the moon after you see it as a full circle?

Moon Changes

The picture cards show how the moon looks at different times. Put them in order. Start with the new moon. Use the pictures to tell how the moon seems to change.

**Day 1
new moon**

**Day 8
quarter moon**

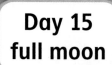

**Day 15
full moon**

Exploring the Moon

In 1969, astronauts went to the moon for the first time. First, they saw the moon's gray dust and craters. A **crater** is a bowl-shaped hole in a surface. Next, the astronauts explored the moon. Later, they brought moon rocks back to Earth.

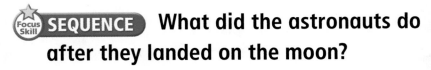 **SEQUENCE** What did the astronauts do after they landed on the moon?

astronaut on the moon

footprint in moon dust

moon rock

Essential Question

What can we observe about the moon?

In this lesson, you learned that the moon seems to change shape in a pattern. You also learned about some things astronauts found and did on the moon.

1.  **SEQUENCE** Make a chart like this one. Tell how the moon changes shape.

2. VOCABULARY Use the word **crater** to talk about this picture.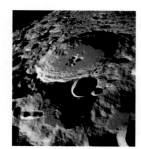

3. DRAW CONCLUSIONS What happens to the moon after you see it as a new moon?

4. SUMMARIZE Use the chart to help you write a summary. Tell about the moon.

Test Prep

5. About how many days is it from one new moon to the next new moon?

A 8   **B** 15

C 22   **D** 29

Make Connections

 Writing

Writing About the Moon
Research what the moon is like. Then write about exploring the moon yourself. What would you want to do and find out? Draw pictures to go with your writing.

I would walk in the craters.

Dr. Mae Jemison

▶ **DR. MAE JEMISON**
▶ Astronaut

From a very young age, Mae Jemison knew that she wanted to be a scientist. She spent hours in the library reading about science topics. Her parents and teachers encouraged her.

After college, she went to medical school and became a doctor. Then she joined the space program. In 1992, she became the first African American woman to go into space. On the mission, she did experiments.

Today, Mae Jemison works with programs to encourage young scientists. She has also written a book to share her experiences.

 Think and Write

Why do you think Mae Jemison did experiments in space?

▶ **DR. FRANKLIN CHANG-DIAZ**

▶ Astronaut

Dr. Franklin Chang-Diaz

One night, a little boy in South America climbed up in a mango tree. He saw a satellite travel across the darkness. He knew then that he wanted to travel in space.

His dream came true. In fact, he was the first Hispanic astronaut. Franklin Chang-Diaz has made seven flights into space. He has gone on three spacewalks.

Franklin Chang-Diaz thinks about the future of space travel. He studies the forces that send rockets into space.

✍ Think and Write

Why might traveling in space be an important job?

375

Vocabulary Review

Choose the correct word to complete each sentence.

sun p. 354   **rotate** p. 362

moon p. 355   **crater** p. 372

1. A word that means to spin is _____.

2. A ball of rock whose light comes from the sun is the _____.

3. The star closest to Earth is the _____.

4. A bowl-shaped hole in the surface of the moon is a _____.

Check Understanding

5. Explain the **effect** when our side of Earth turns toward the sun. Use this picture to help you.

Focus
Skill

6. Which object in the sky gives off its own light?

    A cloud   **C** moon

    B Earth   **D** star

7. Each photo is part of a **sequence**. Which one shows the moon one day after a new moon?

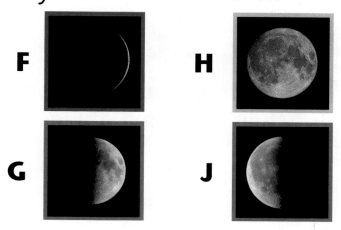

  F   **H**

  G   **J**

Critical Thinking

8. Juan looks at the sky and sees what this picture shows. Tell what you know about each object he sees.

The **Big Idea**

Visual Summary

UNIT D EARTH SCIENCE

Tell how each picture shows the **Big Idea** for its chapter.

CHAPTER 7 Big Idea

We can observe, measure, and describe the weather.

CHAPTER 8 Big Idea

The four seasons all have their own kind of weather.

CHAPTER 9 Big Idea

The sun, moon, and stars are objects in the sky that seem to move because Earth rotates.

PHYSICAL SCIENCE

Slater Mill

Moving water is a force. It can make things work. People have learned to use this force. Slater Mill is one place where water was once used to make things work. It was built along a river at a waterfall. The moving water made machines run. The machines were used to make yarn and cloth from cotton. It was the first textile mill to run on water power.

moving water

turning wheel

yarn made from cotton

The Power of Water

The mill used a water wheel. The flowing water made the wheel turn. The turning wheel made shafts and gears turn. The turning shafts and gears made belts turn. The belts connected the shafts to the machines. At the end of the day, workers shut gates. The gates stopped water from flowing to the wheel.

The Power of Water Today

People still use the power of water. They use it to make lights work in houses and in other buildings. Water provides the power for many things you use each day.

Think And Write

1 **Scientific Thinking** Why is moving water useful to us?

2 **Scientific Thinking** How do people use the power of water today?

Albuquerque International Balloon Fiesta

Can you picture 700 hot-air balloons in the air at the same time? Each October, hot-air balloon pilots from around the world take part in the Albuquerque International Balloon Fiesta. People go to see the balloons and talk to the pilots. They might even take a balloon ride.

balloons at the fiesta

How Does a Hot-Air Balloon Fly?

A hot-air balloon is made of nylon. The basket that people stand in is made of wicker. Above the basket is a burner. The pilot burns fuel. This heats the air inside the balloon. Hot air is less dense than cold air. Cold air pushes up hot air. The hot air fills the balloon and makes it rise. The wind carries the balloon along. The pilot fires the burner from time to time. This reheats the air inside the balloon. The heated air keeps the balloon up in the sky.

air being heated

Think And Write

1. **Scientific Thinking** What makes a hot-air balloon rise upward into the sky?

2. **Scientific Thinking** What happens when the air inside the balloon cools?

Popham Colony and the *Virginia*

caulking iron

In 1607, colonists sailed to America. They sailed from England to what is now the state of Maine. They settled on a river. They built a fort in the first few months. By winter, most of the colonists had left. They sailed back to England. The others stayed until spring. They built a small ship and named it the *Virginia*. It was the first ocean-going ship built by the English in America.

Why a Boat Floats

Have you ever made a boat? Have you ever sailed in a boat? Do you know why a boat floats? It pushes aside the water. The boat takes up the space where the water was. Water also pushes back against the boat. The boat floats because it weighs the same as the water that it pushes aside.

Think And Write

1 **Scientific Thinking** Why does a boat float?

2 **Science and Technology** What are some other things that float in water? What are some things that sink in water? Find out. Use words and pictures to tell what you observed.

canoeing on the river

Project | Spinning Spiral

You need
- big paper circle
- scissors
- string
- pencil

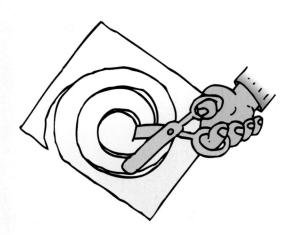

What to Do

❶ Draw a long, curved line on the paper circle. Cut along the line.

❷ Use the pencil to poke a very small hole in the center of the spiral.

❸ Push the string through the hole. Ask an adult to tie a knot.

❹ Hang the paper spiral above a radiator or a lamp. Observe what happens.

Draw Conclusions

❶ What made the paper spiral spin?

❷ What does this tell you about hot air?

Design Your Own Investigation

Sink or Float

Will a ball of clay sink in water? Will clay shaped like a boat float in water? Get some clay, a bowl of water, and paper clips. Plan an investigation to answer the questions. Record what you observe.

UNIT
E
PHYSICAL SCIENCE

Investigating Matter

Unit Inquiry

Water Solutions

As you read this unit, you will find out about things around you. Plan and do a test. Find out what happens to salt when it is mixed with warm or cold water.

All About Matter

What's the Big Idea? Matter can be observed, described, and measured. Heating and cooling can change matter.

GO online Student eBook www.hspscience.com

classifying matter at the beach

What do YOU wonder?

What kinds of matter do you see in this picture? How does this help explain the Big Idea for this chapter?

Investigate to find out ways kinds of matter are alike and different.

Read and Learn about the properties of matter and how it can be sorted.

Fast Fact

Classifying Toys
The largest stuffed bear was 32 feet tall. You can classify toys by size, shape, and color.

matter p. 394

The toys on the shelves are sorted in different ways.

Classify Matter

Ask a Question

How can you classify these objects?
Investigate to find out. Then read and learn to find out more.

Get Ready

Inquiry Skill Tip

When you classify things, you group them by how they are alike. You can draw pictures to show how you classify things.

You need

objects

What to Do

Step ①

Observe the objects.
Compare their sizes,
shapes, and colors.

Step ②

Classify the objects in
three ways.

Step ③

Draw pictures of the
groups you made.

Draw Conclusions

How did you group the
objects?

Independent Inquiry

Go on a rock hunt. Find
four rocks that are very
different. **Classify** the
rocks in two ways.

VOCABULARY
matter

 COMPARE AND CONTRAST
Look for ways matter can be alike and different.

Matter

Everything around you is **matter**. Toys are matter. Balloons are matter. Water is matter, too. Some matter has parts that are too small to see.

What matter do you see here?

All matter is not the same. Matter can be soft or hard. It can be big or small.

Focus Skill **COMPARE AND CONTRAST**

How are the stuffed toy and balloons alike? How are they different?

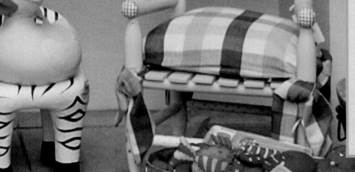

Insta-Lab

Matter Up Close

Observe sand and soil with a hand lens. How are they alike? How are they different? What does the hand lens help you see? Talk to a partner about what you see.

Sorting Matter

You can sort matter. You can sort these objects by color. You can sort them by shape. How else can you sort them?

Focus Skill **COMPARE AND CONTRAST**

How could you sort these objects by color?

Essential Question

What is matter?

In this lesson, you learned that matter has different properties. You also learned that matter can be sorted by these properties.

1. **(Focus Skill) COMPARE AND CONTRAST**
Make a chart like this one. Use it to compare matter.

alike ——— different

2. VOCABULARY Tell about the **matter** in this picture.

3. DRAW CONCLUSIONS How can matter be sorted?

4. SUMMARIZE Write two sentences. Tell how matter can be alike and different.

Test Prep
5. Which is true about matter?

   A It is all the same color.

   B It is all the same size.

   C It is only soft things.

   D Everything is matter.

Make Connections

 Writing

Labeling Matter
Use self-stick notes to make labels for matter in your classroom. On each label, name the matter. Then write three words that tell about it.

book
hard, heavy, purple

pencil
small, yellow, pointed

Investigate to find the masses of different objects.

Read and Learn about the properties of solids and how they can be measured.

Essential Question

What Can We Observe About Solids?

Fast Fact

Toy Lion
This lion is made of toy blocks. You can compare toys in many ways.

toy blocks

399

Measuring Mass

Ask a Question

Compare the bats. Which has more mass? Compare the balls. Which has less mass? Investigate to find out. Then read and learn to find out more.

Get Ready

Inquiry Skill Tip

When you compare, you look for ways things are alike and different. You can write about how you compared the objects.

You need

2 blocks

balance

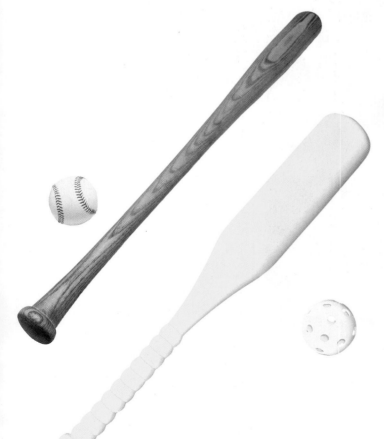

What to Do

Step 1

Put a block on each side of the balance.

Step 2

Look at the blocks on the balance. **Compare.**

Step 3

Which block has more mass? Which has less mass?

Draw Conclusions

How do you know which block has more mass and which has less?

Independent Inquiry

Put two small objects in a bag. Trade with a partner. **Compare** the objects by using your sense of touch.

Observing Solids

How are paper, scissors, and a globe the same? They are all solids.

A **solid** is a kind of matter that keeps its shape. It keeps its shape even when you move it.

Focus Skill MAIN IDEA AND DETAILS

How do you know musical instruments are solids?

403

Mixing Solids

When you mix different kinds of matter together, you make a mixture. A **mixture** is made up of two or more things. These drawing tools make a mixture of solids.

The things in a mixture do not change. You can sort them out of the mixture again.

MAIN IDEA AND DETAILS
What is a mixture made up of?

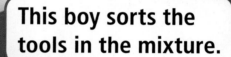

This boy sorts the tools in the mixture.

Insta-Lab

Make Mixtures
Get small things from the classroom. Mix them together. Then trade mixtures with a partner. Sort the things back out of each other's mixtures.

405

Measuring Solids

You can measure solids. You can measure how long a solid is. That is its **length**. You measure length with a ruler.

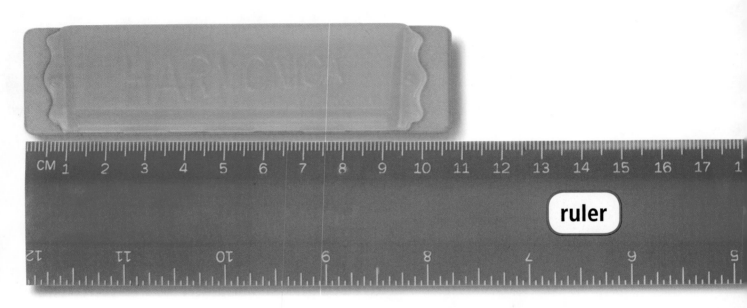

ruler

You can measure the mass of a solid. **Mass** is the amount of matter a solid has. You measure mass with a balance.

Focus Skill MAIN IDEA AND DETAILS What are two ways you can measure solids?

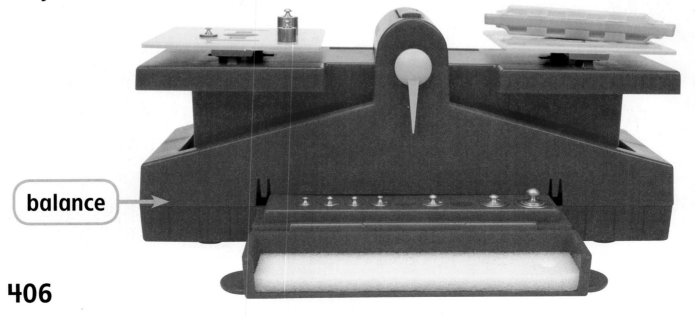

balance

Essential Question

What can we observe about solids?

In this lesson, you learned that a solid keeps its shape when it is moved and that it can be measured. You also learned that mixing solids does not usually change them.

1. 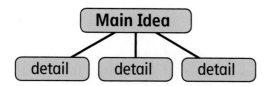 **MAIN IDEA AND DETAILS**
Make a chart like this one. Show details for this main idea. **A solid is matter that keeps its shape.**

```
            Main Idea
         /     |      \
   detail   detail   detail
```

2. VOCABULARY
Tell about the **mass** of these blocks.

3. DRAW CONCLUSIONS How do you know a pencil is a solid?

4. SUMMARIZE Use the vocabulary words to write a summary of the lesson.

Test Prep

5. Write a sentence about two solids you see. Tell how they are alike.

Make Connections

 **Math**

Measure Length
Find three small objects in your classroom. Use paper clips to measure their lengths. Record the lengths in a bar graph. Which object is the longest?

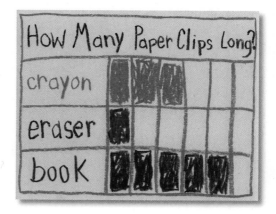

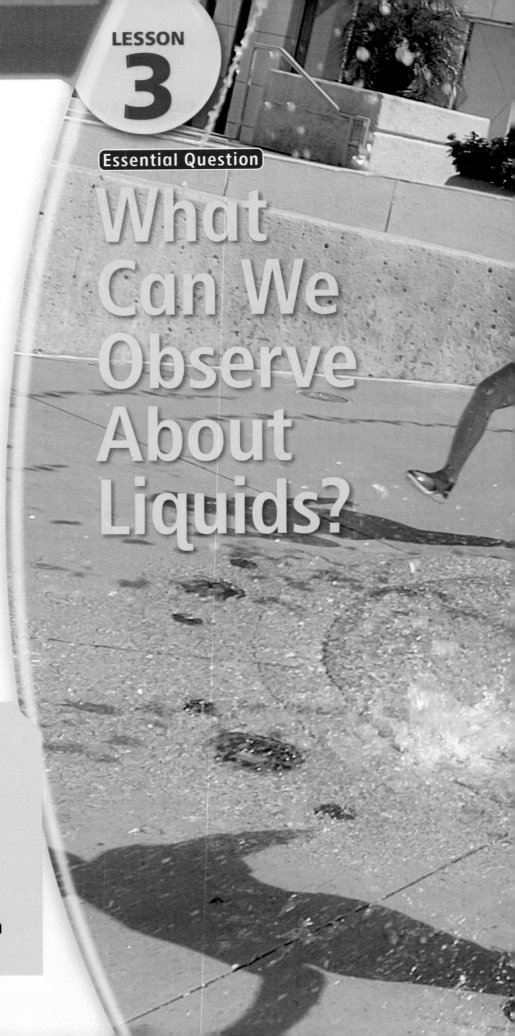

Essential Question

What Can We Observe About Liquids?

Investigate to find out if the amount of liquid in three different containers is the same or different.

Read and Learn about the properties of liquids and how liquids can be measured.

Fast Fact

Measuring Water
Water is all around you. More than half of your body is water! You can measure water with tools.

liquid p. 412

dissolve p. 413

float p. 414

sink p. 415

children running through a fountain

409

The Shape of Liquids

Ask a Question

If you pour juice into these containers, how will the shape of the juice change? Investigate to find out. Then read and learn to find out more.

Get Ready

Inquiry Skill Tip

When you measure, you find the size or amount of something. You can use numbers to record the things you measure.

You need

3 containers of water

measuring cup

What to Do

Step ①

Look at the containers. Draw their shapes.

Step ②

Predict which container will have the most water.

Step ③

Measure the water in each container. Was your prediction right?

Draw Conclusions

How did the shape of the container affect your choice?

Independent Inquiry

Measure spoonfuls of sugar. See how much will completely dissolve in warm water and in cold water. Compare your **measurements.**

Focus Skill **MAIN IDEA AND DETAILS**

Look for main ideas
about liquids.

Observing Liquids

How are the soap and water alike?
Both are liquids.

A **liquid** is matter that flows. It does
not have its own shape. It takes the
shape of its container.

Focus Skill **MAIN IDEA AND DETAILS**

What is a liquid?

liquid
soap

water

Liquid HAND soap

7.5 OZ.

Liquid Mixtures

You can make mixtures with liquids. You can mix drink powder or salt with water. They **dissolve**, or mix completely with the liquid.

If you mix soil or oil with water, they do not dissolve.

 **MAIN IDEA AND DETAILS**

How can you tell if something dissolves?

Mix	Do Not Mix
juice	soil
salt	oil

413

Float and Sink

Does matter float or sink? You can test it.

Some objects **float**, or stay on top of a liquid.

Which objects sink?

Some objects **sink**, or fall to the bottom of a liquid.

(Focus Skill) **MAIN IDEA AND DETAILS**

How can you find out if something floats or sinks?

What Floats?

Get a coin, a pencil, and other classroom objects. Predict which ones will float. Then fill a large bowl with water. Put each object in the water. Were your predictions right?

Measuring Liquids

You can measure liquids. You can use a measuring cup to find out how much space a liquid takes up. You can use a balance to measure its mass.

Focus Skill **MAIN IDEA AND DETAILS**

How can you measure liquids?

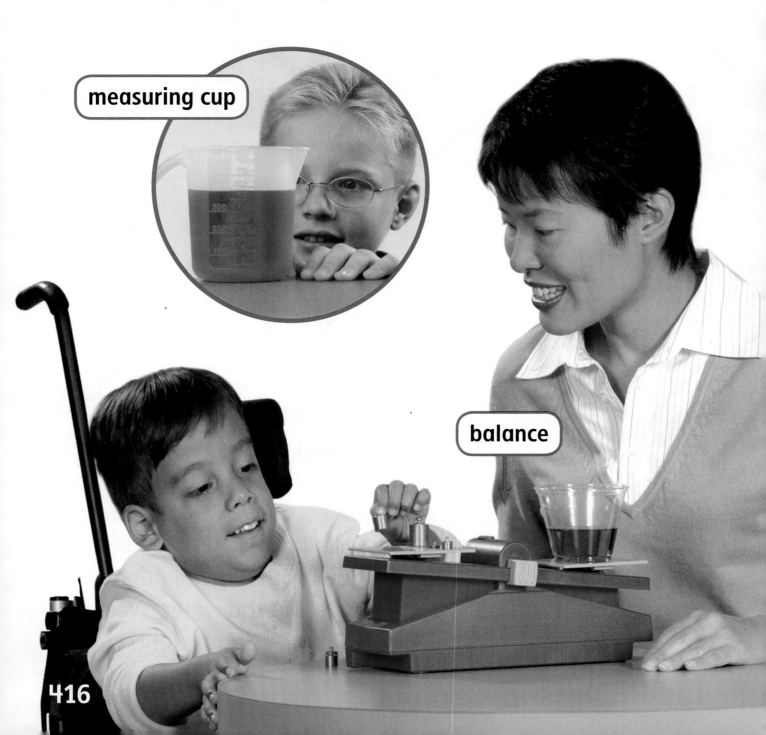

measuring cup

balance

What can we observe about liquids?

In this lesson, you learned that a liquid flows and takes the shape of its container. You also learned that a liquid may be measured by using a measuring cup or a balance.

1. 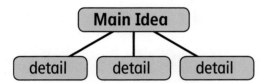 **MAIN IDEA AND DETAILS**
Make a chart like this one. Show details for this main idea. **A liquid is matter that flows.**

Main Idea

detail   detail   detail

2. VOCABULARY
Use the words **sink** and **float** to tell about this picture.

3. DRAW CONCLUSIONS How are solids and liquids alike? How are they different?

4. SUMMARIZE Use the chart to help you write a summary. Tell about liquids.

Test Prep

5. Which tool would you use to measure the mass of a liquid?

A balance   **B** hand lens
C pen   **D** ruler

Make Connections

 Health

Healthful Liquids
Draw pictures of liquids people drink. Sort them into two groups—good for you and not good for you. Talk about why you sorted them as you did.

417

Investigate to find out if there is matter in an empty bottle.

Read and Learn about the properties of gases and how matter can be changed when it is cooled or heated.

Essential Question

What Can We Observe About Gases?

Fast Fact

Bubbles
The biggest bubble ever blown was almost as long as three school buses! Look at this bubble. Infer what is inside it.

Vocabulary Preview

gas p. 423

steam p. 426

girl making a
large bubble

Matter in a Bottle

Ask a Question

These balloons have been made into the shapes of animals. What shape does the air take in each balloon? Investigate to find out. Then read and learn to find out more.

Get Ready

Inquiry Skill Tip

When you infer, you use what you have observed to tell why something happened.

You need

clean plastic bottle

balloon

What to Do

Step ①

Squeeze the bottle.
Blow up the balloon.
Observe the air coming
out of each.

Step ②

Put the balloon in the
bottle. Pull the end around
the top. Try to blow up the
balloon.

Step ③

What happened? **Infer**
what else is in the bottle.

Draw Conclusions

How do you know that
something else is in the
bottle?

Independent Inquiry

Put sugar, yeast, and
warm water in a bag.
Seal and observe. **Infer**
what happened inside
the bag.

VOCABULARY
gas
steam

 **CAUSE AND EFFECT**
Think about how and why matter may change.

Observing Gases

Air is made of gases. A gas is a kind of matter. You can not see most gases.

Where is the air in each picture?

A **gas** is matter that does not have its own shape. It spreads out to fill its container. It takes the shape of the container.

Focus Skill CAUSE AND EFFECT

What would happen if you blew air into a bag? Why?

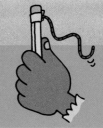

Insta-Lab

A Wind Hunt

Did you know that wind is moving air? Go on a wind hunt. Tape yarn to the end of a pencil. Hold it near heaters, windows, and doors. Observe the yarn. What makes it move?

423

Heating and Cooling Matter

Heating and cooling can change matter. You can see how matter changes by observing water.

In summer, the water in this stream is warm. Being warm keeps the water liquid.

water

In winter, the water in the stream gets cold. When the water gets cold enough, it changes into ice. Ice is solid water.

In spring, the water will get warm again. It will change back into a liquid.

 **CAUSE AND EFFECT**

What changes water from a liquid to a solid?

ice

What Is Steam?

When water boils, it becomes a gas. This gas is called steam.

1 When the water gets hot enough, it becomes steam. The steam goes into the air.

2 As steam cools, it forms tiny drops of water that make a little cloud.

For more links and animations, go to **www.hspscience.com**

Essential Question

What can we observe about gases?

In this lesson, you learned that a gas does not have its own shape and spreads out to fill its container. You also learned that matter can change when it is cooled or heated.

1. 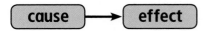 **CAUSE AND EFFECT**
Make a chart like this one. Show what causes some changes in matter.

2. VOCABULARY Use the word **steam** to tell about the picture.

3. DRAW CONCLUSIONS Is ice a gas? How do you know?

4. SUMMARIZE Write three sentences. Tell about gas.

Test Prep
5. Write two sentences to tell how matter can change.

Make Connections

 Art

Make a Mobile
Make a mobile with art supplies, string, and a plastic hanger. Hang it near a window or door. Watch how air moves the objects on the mobile.

427

Manuel Marquez Sanchez

Have you ever opened a milk carton and a bad smell came out? That is because the milk turned sour. Milk turns sour after about 14 days.

A scientist named Manuel Marquez Sanchez has made a new kind of milk carton. This new carton changes color when the milk inside it is turning sour. Sanchez is also trying to make other food packages better.

✎ Think and Write

Why is this new kind of milk carton an important invention?

▶ **MANUEL MARQUEZ SANCHEZ**
▶ Scientist and Inventor

Milk

Joseph Priestley

▶ **JOSEPH PRIESTLEY**

▶ Chemist
▶ Discovered oxygen and other gases

Joseph Priestley was a scientist. He worked on learning about gases. He and another scientist were the first to discover oxygen. Joseph Priestley was the first to show that fire needs oxygen to burn. He also discovered how to use a gas to make water fizz. Joseph Priestley made the world's first glass of soda water!

✎ Think and Write

Why is it important to know that fire needs oxygen to burn?

soda water

Vocabulary Review

Tell which picture goes best with each word.

1. solid p. 403   **3. liquid** p. 412

2. mass p. 406   **4. float** p. 414

A    C

B   D

Check Understanding

5. Tell why this is a mixture.

6. Which is a liquid?

    A air

    B clay

    C milk

    D paper

Critical Thinking

7. What **causes** the stream to change from a solid to a liquid?

8. Think of a solid object. How could you measure it? Write a plan.

Tell how each picture shows the **Big Idea** for the chapter.

CHAPTER **10**

Big Idea

Matter can be observed, described, and measured. Heating and cooling can change matter.

UNIT
F
PHYSICAL SCIENCE

Energy in Our World

Unit Inquiry

Gravity

As you read this unit, you will learn how things move. Plan and do a test. Find out how to make a toy truck go farther.

What's the Big Idea?

Heat, light, and sound are all forms of energy.

Essential Questions

Lesson 1

What Is Heat?

Lesson 2

What Can Light Do?

Lesson 3

What Is Sound?

GO online

Student eBook
www.hspscience.com

Why do musical instruments make different sounds? How do you think this connects to the **Big Idea** for this chapter?

children's marching band

Essential Question

What Is Heat?

Investigate to find out if the sun warms soil faster than air.

Read and Learn about sources of heat and about heat's effect on things.

Fast Fact

The Sun
The sun is made of very, very hot gases. Its heat warms Earth. You can plan an investigation to find out how the sun warms Earth.

heat p. 440

close look at the sun

Heat from the Sun

Ask a Question

What is the sun warming in this picture?
Investigate to find out. Then read and learn to find out more.

Get Ready

Inquiry Skill Tip

When you plan an investigation, you think of what you need to do to test your idea.

You need

cup of soil

2 thermometers

What to Do

Step 1

Does the sun warm soil faster than it warms air? **Plan an investigation** to find out. Write your **plan**.

Step 2

Follow your plan to investigate your ideas.

Step 3

Share with the class what you learned.

Draw Conclusions

Which warmed up faster, the soil or air? Why do you think so? Explain.

Independent Inquiry

Observe some clay. Think about how you could warm it. **Plan an investigation**.

VOCABULARY
heat

CAUSE AND EFFECT
Look for all the effects heat has on things.

Heat

Heat is energy that makes things hot. Heat from the sun warms the land, air, and water all around you.

the sun warming a lake

Some things warm up faster than others. Dark-colored things warm up quickly in the sun. Light-colored things take longer to warm up.

Focus Skill CAUSE AND EFFECT

What can cause something to warm up quickly?

Light and Dark

Make sure two thermometers show the same temperature. Put them under a lamp. Cover one with white paper and one with black paper. Wait 10 minutes. Read the thermometers again. What happened?

Which part of the street gets hot faster?

441

Other Sources of Heat

You can feel heat from other things, too. Fire gives off heat. Lamps and stoves can give off heat. Moving things give off heat, too. Rub your hands together. What do you feel?

Focus Skill CAUSE AND EFFECT

What happens when you rub your hands together?

lamp

fire

stove

friction from rubbing hands

Essential Question

What is heat?

In this lesson, you learned that heat is energy that makes things hot. You also learned that fire, lamps, and stoves give off heat.

1.  **CAUSE AND EFFECT** Make a chart like this one. Show how heat affects things.

cause → effect

2. VOCABULARY Tell about the **heat** in this picture.

3. DRAW CONCLUSIONS What are some things that the sun can warm?

4. SUMMARIZE Use the chart to help you write a summary. Tell about heat.

Test Prep

5. Which things warm up fastest?
  A big things
  B cold things
  C dark-colored things
  D light-colored things

Make Connections

 Writing

Report
Read about the sun. Then write a short report about it. Tell what it is and where it is. Tell what the sun is made of and what it does. Draw pictures to go with your report.

The sun is a star.

443

Investigate to find out why shadows change.

Read and Learn about the properties of light and how shadows are made.

What Can Light Do?

Fast Fact

Shadows

A shadow has a shape like the object that makes it. Draw a conclusion about how shadows are made.

light p. 448

shadow p. 450

shadow of a ballerina

445

Look at Shadows

Guided Inquiry

Ask a Question

Look at the pictures of the sundial. Why do you think the shadow is in a different place in the second picture? Investigate to find out. Then read and learn to find out more.

Get Ready

Inquiry Skill Tip

To draw a conclusion, use what you observe and what you already know to decide what something means.

You need

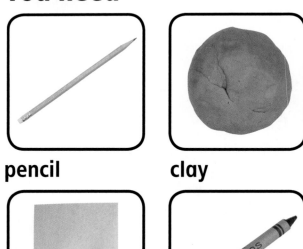

pencil

clay

paper

crayon

What to Do

Step ①

Put a pencil in clay.
Put it on the paper.
Put it in a sunny place.

Step ②

Trace the shadow you see
on the paper.

Step ③

Then trace it at two other
times of the day.

Draw Conclusions

Draw a **conclusion** about
why the shadow changed.

Independent Inquiry

Repeat the Investigate
during the year at the
same time each day.
Draw a **conclusion**
about why the shadow
changed.

VOCABULARY
light
shadow

 **MAIN IDEA AND DETAILS**

Look for main ideas about light and what it does.

Light

Light is a kind of energy. Light from the sun lights up the world around us. Fire and lamps give off light, too. Light lets us see.

sunlight

glass door

closed blinds

Light can move. It can pass through clear objects. It passes through glass. Light can not pass through all objects. Objects that are not clear block light.

 **MAIN IDEA AND DETAILS**
What is the main thing light does for us?

What Can Light Pass Through?

Get some art materials. Predict which ones light will pass through. Which ones will block light? Test your ideas in a sunny place or next to a lamp. **CAUTION:** A lamp may get hot.

449

Shadows

A **shadow** is a dark place made when an object blocks light. You can see many shadows on a sunny day.

MAIN IDEA AND DETAILS

What makes shadows?

shadow

shadow

What can light do?

In this lesson, you learned that light is a kind of energy that lets us see. Light can pass through some objects, but not others. You also learned that shadows are made when objects block light.

1. 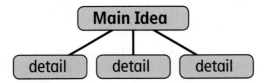 **MAIN IDEA AND DETAILS** Make a chart like this one. Show details for this main idea. **Light is a kind of energy.**

Main Idea

detail   detail   detail

2. VOCABULARY Use the words **light** and **shadow** to tell about this picture.

3. DRAW CONCLUSIONS Do you think all things can make shadows? Explain your answer.

4. SUMMARIZE Use the chart to help you write a summary. Tell about light.

Test Prep

5. Name something that light could pass through. Tell why you think it could.

Make Connections

 **Math**

Measure a Shadow

Measure how tall you are. Record the number. Then go outside. Have a partner measure the shadow of you that the sun makes. Record the number. Compare the numbers. Are they the same?

Essential Question

What Is Sound?

Investigate to find out how sound can make objects move.

Read and Learn about how sounds are made and how they can be different.

Fast Fact

Sound
Sound can travel across spaces. You can hypothesize about what helps sound travel.

sound p. 456

vibrate p. 456

loudness p. 458

pitch p. 459

children singing

453

Watching Sound

Guided Inquiry

Ask a Question

How are these children making sounds? Will the sounds be different? Investigate to find out. Then read and learn to find out more.

Get Ready

Inquiry Skill Tip

When you hypothesize, you tell why you think something will happen. Then you test your idea.

You need

rice

bowl with foil

pan

spoon

What to Do

Step ①

Put a little rice on the foil. **Hypothesize.** Tell what you think will happen to the rice if you make a loud sound.

Step ②

Hold the pan next to the bowl. Tap it once with the spoon. Observe the rice.

Step ③

Was your **hypothesis** right? Talk about it.

Draw Conclusions

Why did the rice move? Explain your answer.

Independent Inquiry

Think about singing into a cardboard tube. How do you think your voice might change? **Hypothesize.**

Focus Skill COMPARE AND CONTRAST

Look for ways sounds can be
alike and different.

How Sounds Are Made

Sound is a kind of energy that
you hear. It is made when something
vibrates. To **vibrate** is to move quickly
back and forth.

What sounds do you
think you could hear
on this street?

When you strum guitar strings, each string vibrates. It makes a sound that you can hear.

COMPARE AND CONTRAST
How are all sounds alike?

vibrating strings

homemade guitar

guitar

Sounds Are Different

Some sounds are soft, and some are loud. A sound's **loudness** is how loud or soft it is. The jet makes a loud sound. What else makes a loud sound?

Whispers are soft sounds.

Jets make loud sounds.

Some sounds are high. Others are low. A sound's **pitch** is how high or low it is. The big bell has a low pitch. What else has a low pitch?

★ Focus Skill COMPARE AND CONTRAST
What is one way sounds may be different?

Straw Instrument

Cut a straw so that the top forms a V. Pinch the top with your lips. Blow very hard. Listen. Then cut some of the bottom off the straw. Blow again. How does the sound change?

Some wind chimes have a high pitch.

A big bell has a low pitch.

459

Musical Instruments

Musical instruments are objects people use to make music. Each kind of instrument causes air to vibrate to make sounds.

When you blow into a trumpet, air vibrates in its metal tubes.

A saxophone has a wooden part called a reed. The reed vibrates, as does the air inside the instrument.

A violin has strings that vibrate.

A drum has a tough cover that vibrates.

For more links and animations, go to **www.hspscience.com**

What is sound?

In this lesson, you learned that sound is a kind of energy that is made when something vibrates. You also learned that sounds can be different because of loudness and pitch.

1. Focus Skill **COMPARE AND CONTRAST**
Make a chart like this one. Use it to compare sounds.

alike —— different

2. VOCABULARY Use the word **vibrate** to tell about the picture.

3. DRAW CONCLUSIONS
What happens to a sound when the vibrations stop?

4. SUMMARIZE Use the vocabulary words to help you write a summary.

Test Prep

5. Which is the word for how high or low a sound is?
   A instrument
   B loudness
   C pitch
   D vibrate

Make Connections

 Music

Voice Vibrations

Your throat has parts that help you talk and sing. Sing high. Sing low. Sing loudly. Sing softly. As you sing, feel your throat. Put your other hand near your lips. Write about what you observe.

How Cell Phones Work

Have you seen kids with cell phones? A cell phone is really a radio. It turns the sound of your voice into another kind of energy. This energy then travels through the air until it reaches a tower.

Dialing Out

The tower picks up the energy. Then the tower sends it to the number you dialed.

The other person's phone turns the energy back into sound. Did you ever think you would be talking so far through the air?

✍️ Think and Write

What does a cell phone do to your voice when you talk into it?

Find out more. Log on to
www.hspscience.com

Vocabulary Review

Match each word to its picture.

1. heat p. 440   **A**

2. light p. 448   **B**

3. shadow p. 450   **C**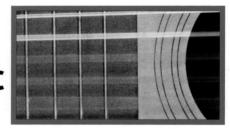

4. vibrate p. 456   **D**

Check Understanding

5. What **causes** some things to warm up faster than others?

6. What kind of clothes are good to wear on a hot day? Tell why.

7. Which kind of pitch does a whistle have?

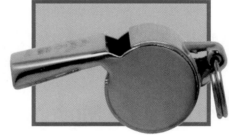

    A high

    B loud

    C low

    D soft

Critical Thinking

8. Look at this musical instrument. What parts vibrate to make sounds? How do you know?

What's the Big Idea?

Objects can move in different ways. Pushes and pulls can cause objects to change speed, direction, and position.

Student eBook
www.hspscience.com

roller coaster

467

Investigate to find out ways kinds of objects can move.

Read and Learn about motion, speed, and the different ways objects can move.

How Do Things Move?

Fast Fact

Blue Angels
The Blue Angels jets move very fast. They also move in many directions as they do tricks. You can classify objects by the ways they move.

Blue Angels

motion p. 472

speed p. 473

469

Ways Objects Move

Guided Inquiry

Ask a Question

Observe the picture of the carousel and the Ferris wheel. How are they moving? Investigate to find out. Then read and learn to find out more.

Get Ready

Inquiry Skill Tip

When you classify things, you group them by how they are alike. You can use pictures or words to show how you classify things.

You need

objects

What to Do

Step ①

Move each object.
Observe the way it moves.

Step ②

Classify the objects by
the ways they move. Then
write about the groups
you made.

Step ③

Talk with classmates about
your groups. Compare
your results.

Draw Conclusions

How do each of the
objects move?

Independent Inquiry

Look around the
classroom. Find objects
that move in different
ways. **Classify** the
objects.

VOCABULARY
motion
speed

COMPARE AND CONTRAST
Look for ways motion and speed can be alike and different.

Motion

Things are in motion all around you. When something is in **motion**, it is moving. What is moving here?

jump rope

race car

Objects move at different speeds. **Speed** is how fast something moves. Both of these objects are moving. They are not moving at the same speed. Which is moving faster?

Focus Skill COMPARE AND CONTRAST

How can speeds of objects be different?

tricycle

Insta-Lab

Motion Graph

Test some toys. Do they move in a straight path, a curved path, a circle, or a zigzag? Record. Then make a bar graph to show how many toys move in each way.

How Objects Move							
straight line							
curve							
circle							
zigzag							
	0	1	2	3	4	5	6	7

473

How Things Move

Things may move in different ways. An object may move in a straight path. It may move in a curved path. It may go in a circle. It may even move in a zigzag.

Focus Skill COMPARE AND CONTRAST

What are some different ways an object can move?

zigzag

curved path

circle

straight path

How do things move?

In this lesson, you learned that things in motion are moving and that speed is how fast things move. You also learned that objects can move in a straight path, curved path, circle, or zigzag.

1. **COMPARE AND CONTRAST** Make a chart like this one. Use it to compare motion.

2. VOCABULARY Tell about the **motion** in this picture.

3. DRAW CONCLUSIONS How is motion different from speed?

4. SUMMARIZE Use the chart to help you write a summary. Tell about motion.

Test Prep

5. What are some different ways objects can move?

Make Connections

✏ Writing

Write About Motion
Think of a sport or an active game you like to play. How do you move your body? Write a description. Tell how your body moves when you play.

I play soccer. I run in a zigzag.

Investigate to find out how objects can be moved by using pushes and pulls.

Read and Learn how forces, such as pushes and pulls, can change the way objects move.

How Can You Change the Way Things Move?

Fast Fact

Juggling

This man is a juggler. He can juggle 3 pins at a time. You can plan an investigation to find out ways to make objects move.

man juggling pins

Vocabulary Preview

force p. 480

push p. 481

pull p. 481

477

Pulling and Pushing Objects

Ask a Question

Observe the pictures. What force is being used in each picture?
Investigate to find out. Then read and learn to find out more.

Get Ready

Inquiry Skill Tip

When you plan an investigation, you think of what you need to do to test your idea.

You need

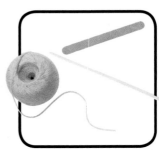

small cube

objects to make cube move

What to Do

Step ❶

Look at the objects.
How can you use them
to push or pull the cube?
Plan an investigation.

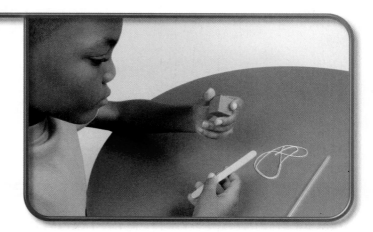

Step ❷

Follow your **plan**.
Tell how you moved the
cube. Use the words **push**
and **pull**.

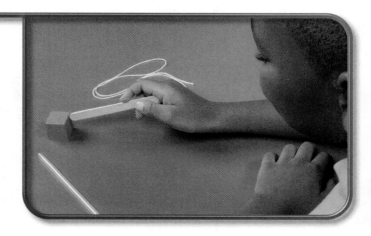

Step ❸

Repeat your **plan**. Do you
get the same results?

Draw Conclusions

How did you use the
objects to make the cube
move?

Independent Inquiry

What can change the
speed and direction
of a marble? **Plan an
investigation.**

VOCABULARY

force   pull
push

 **CAUSE AND EFFECT**

Look for actions that cause objects to move.

Making Things Move

A **force** makes something move or stop moving. You use force each time you move an object. You use force to move your body, too.

Pushes and pulls are forces. When you **push** an object, you move it away from you. When you **pull** an object, you move it closer to you.

CAUSE AND EFFECT

What happens when you push an object?

pulling

pushing

481

Changing Speed

You use force to change the speed of an object. These balls are moving very fast. You can push to stop a ball. Then you can pull it close. You can also push it away by kicking to make it move faster.

 **CAUSE AND EFFECT**

What can cause a ball to move faster?

pushing away

pulling toward

482

Changing Direction

You use force to change an object's direction. When you play baseball, the ball moves toward you. Then you hit it with the bat. Hitting the ball is a push. The ball moves away from you.

(Focus Skill) CAUSE AND EFFECT
What happens to a ball when you hit it?

Push and Pull a Ball
Play ball with your classmates. Throw and kick a ball to one another. Each time you touch the ball, tell whether you use a push or a pull.

What force does the boy use to change the ball's direction?

Changing Position

You use force to change where an object is. You can push a toy truck inside the station and pull it outside. You can use force to move an object above or below another object. You can use force to move the orange car to the left of or the right of the red post.

Focus Skill **CAUSE AND EFFECT** How can you change where an object is?

above and below

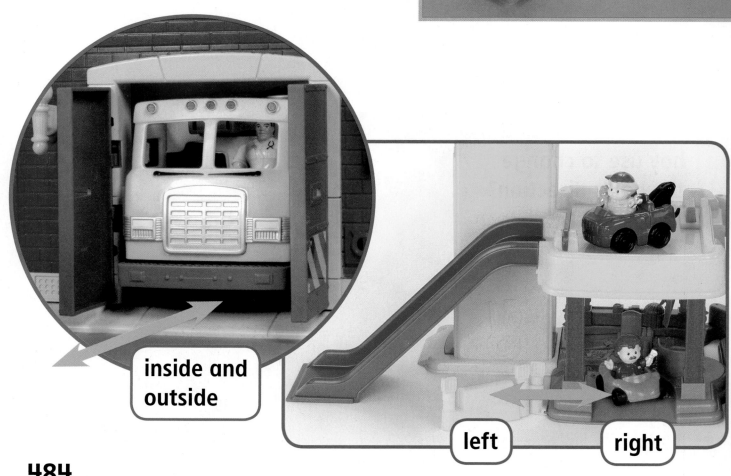

inside and outside

left

right

484

How can you change the way things move?

In this lesson, you learned that pushes and pulls can change an object's speed, direction, and position.

1. **Focus Skill** CAUSE AND EFFECT Make a chart like this one. Show how force affects motion.

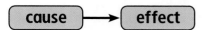

2. VOCABULARY Use the word **push** to tell about the picture.

3. DRAW CONCLUSIONS What force do you use when you jump?

4. SUMMARIZE Use the vocabulary words to help you write a summary of the lesson.

Test Prep

5. Write a sentence about what causes objects to move or stop moving.

Make Connections

 **Math**

Adding to Keep Score

In some games, players push objects to score points. Make your own pushing game. Use a box lid. Push a bottle cap from one end to score points. Do this 3 times. Add your points to find your score.

Essential Question

How Does Gravity Make Things Move?

Investigate to find out how a ball will move.

Read and Learn about how gravity affects objects.

Fast Fact

Gravity
Gravity pulls your body down a slide. You can predict how gravity will move an object.

gravity p. 490

gravity pulling a
girl down the slide

487

How a Ball Will Move

Ask a Question

What is causing these leaves to fall? Investigate to find out. Then read and learn to find out more.

Get Ready

Inquiry Skill Tip

When you predict, you use what you know to make a guess about what will happen.

You need

tape

ball

ramp

What to Do

Step 1

Set up the ramp. **Predict** where the ball will stop when you roll it down the ramp. Mark the spot with tape.

Step 2

Roll the ball down the ramp.

Step 3

Was your **prediction** correct? Talk about what you found out.

Draw Conclusions

What do you think would happen if you made the ramp higher?

Independent Inquiry

Does gravity pull liquids? **Predict** what will happen. Investigate. Was your **prediction** correct?

VOCABULARY
gravity

CAUSE AND EFFECT
Look for the effect gravity has on objects.

Gravity Makes Things Move

Gravity is a force that pulls things straight down to the ground. Gravity makes things fall unless something is holding them up.

Look at the diver. Nothing is holding her up. Which way will she move? The diver will move down because of gravity.

CAUSE AND EFFECT What effect does gravity have on objects?

diver

dog food

What is gravity moving here?

sled

Insta-Lab

Falling Objects

Watch the way gravity pulls different things down. Your teacher will drop a ball and a pencil from high up. Observe how they fall. Why do you think this happened?

491

How Things Fall

Gravity moves all objects on Earth the same way. It pulls them straight down. A push or a pull can change an object's path. A push or a pull can hold an object up. If there are no pushes or pulls, all objects fall.

The ball is light. The rock is heavy.

The boy drops the ball and the rock at the same time.

Both fall and land at the same time.

For more links and animations, go to **www.hspscience.com**

Essential Question

How does gravity make things move?

In this lesson, you learned that gravity pulls objects straight down to the ground. You also learned that objects fall unless something holds them up.

1. ⭐(Focus Skill) **CAUSE AND EFFECT**
Make a chart like this one. Show how gravity affects motion.

cause ⟶ effect

2. VOCABULARY Use the word **gravity** to tell about this picture.

3. DRAW CONCLUSIONS
What happens when two different objects are dropped from the same height at the same time?

4. SUMMARIZE Use the chart to help you write a summary. Tell about gravity.

Test Prep
5. How could you stop gravity from pulling a ball to the ground?

Make Connections

 Physical Education

Exercise

In some kinds of exercise, you push against gravity. Draw pictures that show how you exercise. Label the body parts you use to push against gravity. Then show your exercises to a partner.

I push with my feet.

493

Investigate to find out what kinds of objects magnets can move.

Read and Learn about magnets and magnetic force.

Essential Question

How Do Magnets Make Things Move?

Fast Fact

Magnets
This magnet is very strong. It can pick up recycled steel. You can hypothesize about what a magnet will pull.

large magnet picking
up recycled steel

magnet p. 498

attract p. 498

**magnetic
force** p. 500

pole p. 502

repel p. 502

What Magnets Pull

Ask a Question

Look at the picture. What is holding the lid to the can opener?
Investigate to find out. Then read and learn to find out more.

Get Ready

Inquiry Skill Tip

When you hypothesize, you tell what you think will happen. Then test your idea.

You need

bar magnet

objects

What to Do

Step 1

Look at the objects. Which ones will a magnet pull? **Hypothesize**.

Step 2

Test your **hypothesis**. Use a magnet. Record your observations.

What a Magnet Can Do		
Object	Pulls	Does Not Pull

Step 3

Was your **hypothesis** correct? How do you know?

Draw Conclusions

Would you get the same results if you repeated the Investigate? Explain.

Independent Inquiry

Where are the poles on a magnet? **Hypothesize**. Investigate and record your observations.

VOCABULARY

magnet   pole
attract   repel
magnetic force

MAIN IDEA AND DETAILS
Find out what magnets are and how they move objects.

Magnets

A **magnet** is an object that will **attract**, or pull, things made of iron.

magnets

498

What does a magnet attract?
You can test objects to see. A magnet
does not attract all metals. It attracts
metals that have iron in them. Steel
has iron in it.

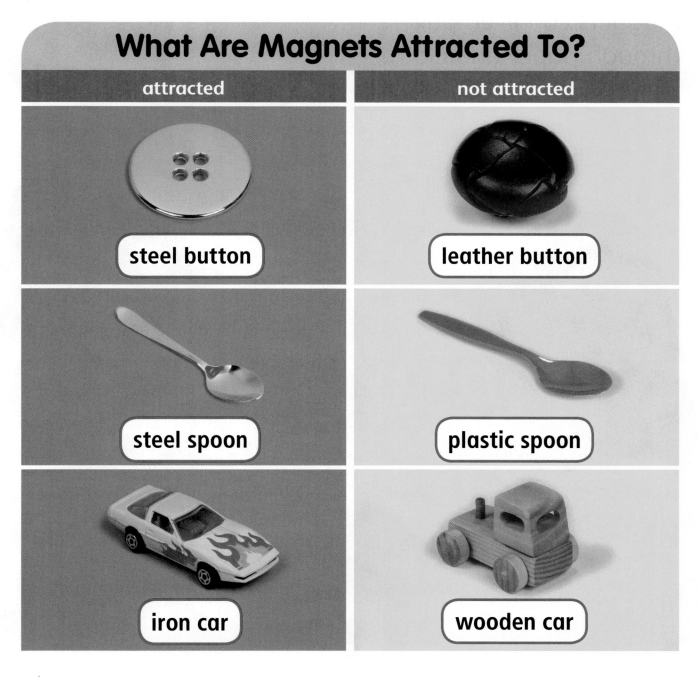

What Are Magnets Attracted To?

attracted	not attracted
steel button	leather button
steel spoon	plastic spoon
iron car	wooden car

 **MAIN IDEA AND DETAILS**

What is a magnet?

Force of a Magnet

A magnet's pull is called **magnetic force**. Some magnets have a lot of force. They are very strong. Many magnets can even pull through paper and cloth.

magnet pulling through paper

magnet pulling without touching

Magnets attract objects without touching them. Strong ones can pull from far away. This magnet pulls a paper clip on a kite when it is held above it.

★ Focus Skill **MAIN IDEA AND DETAILS**
How do you know if a magnet has a strong magnetic force?

Insta-Lab

Move It with a Magnet
Find out what a magnet pulls through. Use a strong magnet. Try to attract a metal clip through paper, cloth, and other materials. Tell what you observe.

501

Poles of a Magnet

A magnet has an N pole and an S pole. A **pole** is near an end of a bar magnet. The pull is strongest at a magnet's poles.

You can try to put magnets together. If the poles are different, they attract each other. Poles that are the same **repel** each other, or push each other away.

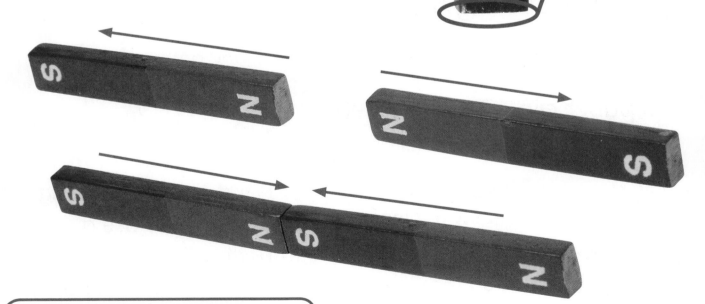

MAIN IDEA AND DETAILS

What are a magnet's poles?

poles

What happens when you try to put magnets together?

Essential Question

How do magnets make things move?

In this lesson, you learned about objects magnets attract and about magnetic force. You also learned that magnets have two poles that can attract or repel each other.

1. 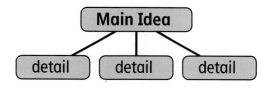 **MAIN IDEA AND DETAILS**
Make a chart like this one. Show details for this main idea. **A magnet is an object that attracts things made of iron.**

Main Idea

detail   detail   detail

2. VOCABULARY Use the word **attract** to tell about the picture.

3. DRAW CONCLUSIONS
What can you tell about a toy that a magnet attracts?

4. SUMMARIZE Use the vocabulary words to write a summary of the lesson.

Test Prep

5. Which thing happens if you put together two poles that are the same?
   A They attract.
   B They pull.
   C They break.
   D They repel.

Make Connections

 Social Studies

Recycling with Magnets
Recycling centers use magnets to sort kinds of metal. See how. Get clean pieces of metal from a recycling bin. Use a magnet to sort them. Make a chart to show your groups.

has iron	does not have iron
jar lid	soda can

503

Making Driving Safer

Driving on roads now is always risky. Drivers need to be more careful than ever. One kind of car has a new safety system. The system helps keep drivers from getting into an accident.

When the car gets too close to another car, the system tells the driver to slow down. It makes a buzzing sound and flashes the word BRAKE. The system buzzes and flashes until the driver slows down. The system also gently pulls on the driver's seatbelt. This alerts the driver. It holds the driver more tightly if there is an accident, too.

Vocabulary Review

Choose the word that best completes each sentence.

speed p. 473   **magnet** p. 498

gravity p. 490   **repel** p. 502

1. For a magnet, to push away is to _____.

2. An object that attracts things made of iron is a _____.

3. A force that pulls things to the ground is _____.

4. How fast an object moves is its _____.

Check Understanding

5. Use these pictures to **compare** different ways objects can move.

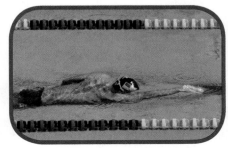

6. Look at this picture. What force is
causing the sled to move?

A gravity

B magnetic force

C N and S poles

D speed

Critical Thinking

7. Why do you think magnets stick to most refrigerators?

8. List these objects in order from slowest to fastest.

The Big Idea

A

B

C

Visual Summary

Tell how each picture shows the **Big Idea** for its chapter.

CHAPTER 11 Big Idea

Heat, light, and sound are all forms of energy.

CHAPTER 12 Big Idea

Objects can move in different ways. Pushes and pulls can cause objects to change speed, direction, and position.

Visit the Multimedia Science Glossary to see illustrations of these words and to hear them pronounced.
www.hspscience.com

A glossary lists words in alphabetical order. To find a word, look it up by its first letter or letters.

 A

adaptation

A body part or behavior that helps a living thing. (150)

amphibian

A kind of animal that has smooth, wet skin. (72)

attract

To pull something. A magnet attracts things made of iron. (498)

B

beach

Flat sandy land along a shore. (220)

bird

The only kind of animal that has feathers. (71)

crater

A hole in a surface that is shaped like a bowl. The moon has many craters. (372)

C

camouflage

A kind of adaptation where an animal's color or pattern helps it hide. (154)

D

desert

Land that gets very little rain. (184)

condense

To change from water vapor into tiny water drops. The drops form clouds. (300)

dissolve

To completely mix a solid with a liquid. (413)

drought

A long time with little rain that causes the land to get very dry. (235)

 E

edible

Safe to eat. (126)

environment

All the things that are in a place. (142)

erosion

When moving water changes the land by carrying rocks and soil to new places. (236)

evaporate

To change from liquid into water vapor. (300)

 F

fall

The season after summer when the air begins to get cooler. (332)

fish

A kind of animal that is covered in scales, uses gills to take in oxygen, and lives in water. (73)

float

To stay on top of a liquid. (414)

flood

When rivers and streams get too full and the water flows onto land. (234)

flowers

The parts of a plant that make fruits. (108)

food chain

A diagram that shows how animals and plants are linked by what they eat. (164)

force

Something that makes an object move or stop moving. (480)

forest

Land that is covered with trees. (176)

fruits

The parts of a plant that hold the seeds. (108)

 G

gas

A kind of matter that does not have its own shape. (423)

gills

The parts of a fish that take in oxygen from the water. (63)

gravity

A force that pulls things down to the ground. (490)

H

habitat

The place where an animal finds food, water, and shelter. (178)

heat

A kind of energy that makes things hotter. (440)

hill

A high place that is smaller than a mountain and usually round on top. (217)

humus

Pieces of dead plants and animals. Humus, clay, and sand make up soil. (258)

 I

inquiry skills

The skills people use to find out information. (20)

insect

A kind of animal that has three body parts and six legs. (74)

 L

lake

A body of water with land around most of it. (227)

larva

Another name for a caterpillar. (82)

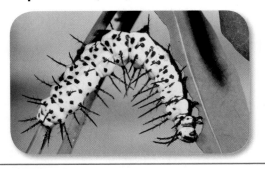

leaves

The parts of a plant that take in light and air to make food. (107)

length

The measure of how long a solid is. (406)

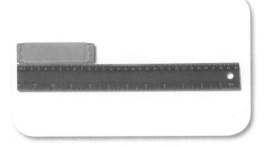

life cycle

All the parts of a plant's or animal's life. (80)

light

A kind of energy that lets us see. (448)

liquid

A kind of matter that flows and takes the shape of its container. (412)

living

Needing food, water, and air to grow and change. (54)

loudness

How loud or soft a sound is. (458)

lungs

The parts of some animals that help them breathe air. Pigs are animals that use lungs to breathe. (63)

 M

magnet

An object that will attract things made of iron. (498)

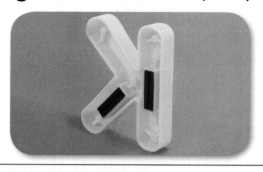

magnetic force

The pulling force of a magnet. (500)

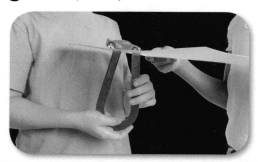

mammal

A kind of animal that has hair or fur and feeds its young milk. (70)

mass

The measure of how much matter something has. You can measure mass with a balance. (406)

matter

Everything around you. Matter can be a solid, liquid, or gas. (394)

migrate

To move to a new place to find food. (334)

mixture

Two or more things that have been mixed together. (404)

moon

A huge ball of rock in the sky that does not give off its own light. (355)

motion

When something is moving. Things are in motion when they move. (472)

mountain

The highest kind of land, with sides that slope toward the top. (216)

natural resource

Anything from nature that people can use. (248)

nonedible

Describes something that is not safe to eat. (127)

nonliving

Not needing food, water, and air and not growing. (55)

nutrients

Minerals in the soil that plants need to grow and stay healthy. (98)

ocean

A large body of salt water. (192, 228)

oxygen

A kind of gas that plants give off and animals need to breathe. People need trees to get oxygen. (161)

pitch

How high or low a sound is. (459)

plain

Flat land that spreads out a long way. (218)

pole

Near an end of a magnet where the pull is strongest. (502)

pollen

A powder that flowers need to make seeds. Bees help carry pollen from one flower to another. (162)

pollution

Waste that causes harm to land, water, or air. (266)

R11

pull

To tug an object closer to you. (481)

pupa

The part of a life cycle when a caterpillar changes into a butterfly. (82)

push

To press an object away from you. (481)

recycle

To use old resources to make new things. (269)

reduce

To use less of a natural resource. (268)

repel

To push away. Poles that are the same on a magnet repel each other. (502)

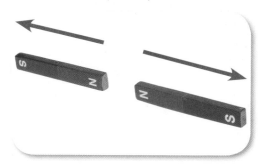

reptile

A kind of animal that has scaly, dry skin. (72)

reuse

To use a natural resource again. (269)

river

A large body of moving water. (226)

rock

A hard, nonliving thing that comes from Earth. (256)

roots

The parts of a plant that hold it in the soil and take in water and nutrients. (105)

rotate

To spin around like a top. Earth rotates and causes day and night. (362)

S

science tools

The tools that help scientists find what they need. (30)

season

A time of year. The seasons are spring, summer, fall, and winter. (314)

seed coat

A covering that protects a seed. (114)

seeds

The parts of a plant that new plants grow from. (108)

senses

The way we tell what the world is like. The five senses are sight, hearing, smell, taste, and touch. (6)

shadow

A dark place made when an object blocks light. (450)

shelter

A place where animals can be safe. (64)

sink

To fall to the bottom of a liquid. (415)

soil

The top layer of Earth, made of sand, humus, and clay. (258)

solid

A kind of matter that keeps its shape. (403)

sound

A kind of energy that you hear. (456)

speed

The measure of how fast something moves. (473)

spring

The season after winter when the weather gets warmer. (316)

star

An object in the sky that gives off its own light. (354)

steam

Gas that comes from boiling water. (426)

stem

The part of a plant that holds up the plant and lets food and water move through the plant. (106)

stream

A small body of moving water that flows downhill. (226)

summer

The season after spring that is usually hot. Summer has many hours of daylight. (324)

sun

The star closest to Earth. (354)

sunlight

Light that comes from the sun. (97)

tadpole

A young frog that comes out of an egg and has gills to take in oxygen. (80)

temperature

The measure of how hot or cold something is. You can measure temperature with a thermometer. (292)

thermometer

A tool used to measure temperature. (292)

valley

The low land between mountains or hills. (218)

vibrate

To move quickly back and forth. (456)

water cycle

The movement of water from Earth to the air and back again. (300)

water vapor

Water in the air that you can not see. (300)

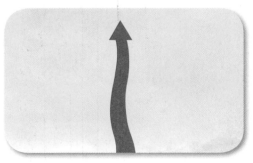

weather

What the air outside is like. (284)

winter

The season after fall that is usually cold. Winter has the fewest hours of daylight. (340)

Index

CHARACTERISTIC Giraffes are the tallest land-living animals in the world.

YOUNG A baby giraffe is called a calf.

CHARACTERISTIC Giraffes have a blue-black tongue.

DIET Giraffes feed on leaves, twigs, and fruits from trees and bushes.